FORT STANTON

and Its Community
1855–1896

JOHN P. RYAN

YUCCA TREE PRESS
LAS CRUCES, NEW MEXICO

First Printing August 1998
Second Printing July 2003

Cover and book design by Vicki Ligon, Barbed Wire Publishing

Ryan, John P.
    FORT STANTON AND ITS COMMUNITY, 1855–1896.
        1. Southwest United States—History. 2. New Mexico, Territory of—
        History. 3. United States—Indian Wars.
        I. John P. Ryan.   II. Title

ISBN: 1-881325-28-8

Table of Contents

List of Illustrations

MAPS

The revised edition of *Fort Stanton and Its Community* is a joint effort of Barbed Wire Publishing, Fort Stanton, Inc., and the author. Fort Stanton, Inc. is a not-for-profit organization dedicated to the promotion and preservation of Fort Stanton, NM and its history. Revenues from books sold through the efforts of Fort Stanton, Inc. go directly to their preservation projects. Barbed Wire Publishing distributes the book to national and regional booksellers, libraries, museums, and schools outside of the immediate area surrounding Lincoln and Fort Stanton, NM.

Fort Stanton's parade grounds today. *Courtesy of author.*

Acknowledgments

I wish to gratefully acknowledge the assistance of the many people who so generously assisted me during the writing of this manuscript.

Foremost is the understanding and support of my wife, Margaret.

Special thanks goes to Professor Darlis A. Miller. Without her suggestions and guidance, this work would not have been possible.

The staff of the New Mexico State University library, especially Karen George of government documents, Tim Blevins of the archives, and Cheryl Wilson of special collections gave indispenable help. Al Regensberg of the New Mexico State Archives and Records Center provided considerable assistance in locating information and documents. Mr. Art Olivas of the Museum of New Mexico went to extra lengths to provide photographs.

Ann Buffington, Cindy Martinez, Colleen Salazar, and Dori Salazar of the Lincoln County Heritage Trust Museum generously allowed me full use of the museum's facilities and helped considerably with locating documents. I also wish to thank Sandra McFadden of the Fort Stanton Adult Rehabilitation Facility who made it possible to visit and photograph the original buildings at Fort Stanton. Judi M. Morris provided an informative and thorough tour of the historical parts of the fort.

Jerry W. Ballard of the Bureau of Land Management escorted me though the Fort Stanton cave and facilitated efforts to photograph artifacts in the cave.

Many thanks to my family and friends for their support, particularly Kathy and Aubrey Thompson, for allowing me to impose upon them during my many trips to Albuquerque and Santa Fe.

Finally, I would like to thank Nisha Hoffman who assisted me in the review of materials for the revised edition.

Any mistakes in this book are entirely my own.

John Ryan
Las Cruces, NM

Introduction

In 1848, representatives of the United States and Mexico signed the Treaty of Guadalupe Hidalgo, ending the war between the two countries. This treaty ceded to the United States the vast territory of New Mexico. But it also gave the United States the responsibility for preventing the Indians in this territory from raiding into Mexico. The Gadsden Purchase of 1853 relieved the United States of that obligation, but by then the Army was engaged in an intermittent war of conquest with the Indians of the Southwest that would last for nearly forty years. The Army placed posts at strategic locations throughout the territory to control the Indians. The government expected these posts to protect settlers and encourage more people to homestead in the region. In keeping with that policy, Army posts provided assistance when needed, including food and necessities when times were bad.[1]

The Army built some of the military posts in New Mexico adjacent to substantial communities, such as Fort Marcy near Santa Fe and Fort Fillmore near Mesilla. However, commanders situated many posts in outlying areas and some—such as Forts Massachusetts, Stanton, and Defiance—were in very remote locations. These posts were more important to the settlement of their localities than posts in less isolated areas because no previous homesteading had occurred in their vicinity. Due to great distances and lack of roads, supply was slow and transportation costs prohibitive, making these remote posts difficult and expensive to supply. The isolated forts found it much cheaper and more efficient, as settlers came under their aegis, to purchase what goods and services they could from the nearby settlers. Even after the Army built roads to supply the forts, the trading relationship continued. A kind of symbiosis had developed between the isolated forts and the communities surrounding them. Additionally, the new roads, built primarily for military purposes, opened commerce to the regions surrounding the posts.[2]

The object of this book is not only to bring to light significant events in the history of Fort Stanton itself, but to describe the develop-

Fort Stanton as it appears today. *Courtesy of author.*

ment and collapse of the symbiotic relationship between the fort and the community it served. To accomplish its objective, this book will examine the way in which the fort, by providing protection and assistance to the settlers and a market for their produce, fostered settlement and growth in the region while the community, by providing needed goods and services, supported the fort. This relationship dissolved as the Indian wars came to an end, the community expanded, and communications improved.

Notes to the Introduction

1. Darlis A. Miller, *The Frontier Army in the Far West: 1860–1900*, (St. Louis, Mo.: Forum Press, 1979) pp. 1–2.

2. Robert W. Frazer, *Forts and Supplies: The Role of the Army in the Economy of the Southwest, 1846–1861*, (Albuquerque: University of New Mexico Press, 1983) pp. 114–120.

Chapter I

THE EARLY YEARS

Indians had been raiding, killing, and stealing in southern New Mexico since settlement of the region began. In 1851, and again in 1852, the government signed treaties with various bands, but these treaties did not have any lasting effect. By 1854, the raids had reached serious proportions. On Christmas day, 1854, a combined force of Ute and Jicarilla Indians raided and destroyed the town of Pueblo on the Arkansas River. To bolster the army forces in the area, General John Garland, the military commander for the Department of New Mexico, and New Mexico Acting Governor David Meriwether called up five companies of territorial volunteers, composed primarily of Hispanics. Ceran St.Vrain, commissioned as Lieutenant Colonel, commanded the volunteers.[1]

On the morning of January 5, 1855, a large force—eighty men, three officers, forty mules, eight Hispanic packers, one guide and one interpreter—with Capt. Henry W. Stanton in command, set out from Fort Fillmore in pursuit of a band of Mescalero Apaches who had stolen some 2,500 sheep and disappeared into the Sierras in the vicinity of White Mountain. Captain Stanton was to join, or communicate with, a force commanded by Capt. Richard S. Ewell out of Fort Thorn by the fifteenth of January. Stanton was instructed to "...attack any party of Indians he may fall in with having sheep or cattle...." Stanton and Ewell met on January seventh and camped near the Rio Peñasco. Ewell's troops thought they had seen an Indian running in the bushes on the afternoon of the seventh, so they began a systematic patrol of the area. On the night of the ninth, the troop's horses were spooked by something or someone. Indians were suspected, but while the soldiers continued to find sign, they found no Indians.

On the night of the eighteenth, the soldiers' camp was attacked by Indians who stole the horses and set fire to the grass surrounding the camp.[2] At dawn, January 19, the troops awoke to the taunts of a band of Indians dancing around a fire on the hillside. The soldiers saddled up without breakfast and went after them. The main force attacked along the banks of the Rio Peñasco, while small parties of dragoons sortied after various groups of Indians. This running fight lasted until about four o'clock that afternoon. While the main body of soldiers set up camp for the evening, Captain Stanton led a detail of twelve men into a deep ravine where Indians waited in ambush. When the troops in camp heard gunfire they rushed to support Stanton's small force. A hard fight ensued but it lasted only twenty minutes before the Indians fled the scene. Stanton, trying to cover his men's retreat, had been shot in the forehead and died instantly. Privates Thomas Dwyer and John Hennings were also killed in the ambush. The soldiers buried the bodies, wrapped in blankets, and built fires over the graves to hide the location until they could recover them on their return trip.[3]

Four days later, as the now bedraggled troops returned from chasing Indians throughout the mountainous terrain, they stopped to recover the remains of those killed on the nineteenth. Someone had disinterred the corpses and taken the blankets. Animals had mutilated the bodies and the corpses were in bad condition. While the troops rested their horses and pack animals, the soldiers put the bodies on piles of wood and burned the flesh off the bones. The expedition then took the remains back to Fort Fillmore for a proper military funeral. The returning expedition, led by Captain Ewell, reached Fort Fillmore on February 2. Stanton's wife waited over an hour at her front door for her husband before a soldier informed her of his death. The garrison interred the remains of Captain Stanton, Private Dwyer, and Private Hennings the next day, February 3, with full military honors.[4]

In response to the incident on the Rio Peñasco, General John Garland took forceful action against the Mescalero people. In March 1855, General Garland sent out two columns with three months' sup-

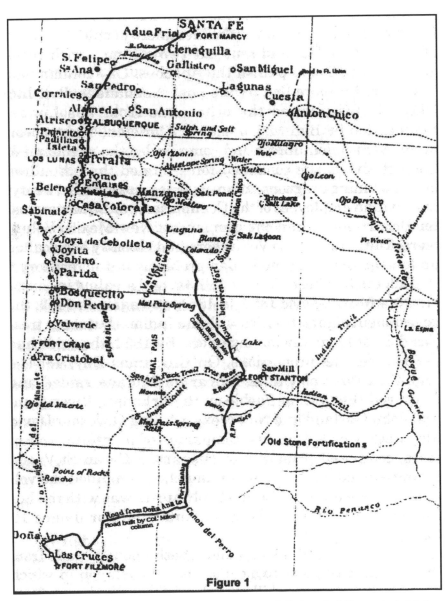

Figure 1

Roads built by the converging columns of Colonel Miles and Major Carleton on their March 1855 punitive expedition to punish the Mescalero Apaches following the death of Captain Stanton (adapted from the atlas to accompany *The Official Records of the Union and Confederate Armies, 1861–1865*, Part I, plate 54, map 1).

3

plies to punish the Apaches. One column was from Fort Fillmore, led by the post commander, Bvt. Ltc. Dixon S. Miles, and the other was from Los Lunas, commanded by Bvt. Maj. James H. Carleton. The two columns were to join forces and come under the command of Colonel Miles. The combined force totaled three hundred men, including dragoons, infantry, spies and guides, twenty-five civilian employees of the commissary and quartermaster departments, and one company of New Mexico Volunteers. The New Mexico Volunteers had recently been called up to help deal with the Indian problems in the territory.[5]

Carleton's and Miles' columns both opened roads from their respective posts to a camp near the canyon in which Captain Stanton was killed, known as James Canyon today. The campsite was located on a wide path at a point where the Apaches forded the Peñasco and Pajaro rivers, about four hundred yards from the banks of the Peñasco. Miles speculated that the Apaches used this path frequently when they were going out to raid and pillage. The camp was situated in an area that Miles described as bottomland, rich and good for farming. He named it "Camp Stanton" in honor of the slain officer.[6]

Miles' force promptly began operations against the Apache, but saw little action before the fighting ended. On April 2, 1855, the Apaches, cornered in Dog Canyon, sued for peace. Miles, who had sent Captain Stanton on his fatal mission, was strongly tempted to take advantage of a rare opportunity to severely punish the Indians. However, his sense of fair play prevailed and he honored the white flag. Indian agent Dr. Michael Steck pleaded the Indians' cause and, in May, New Mexico Territory's Governor David Meriwether signed a treaty with them. The treaty was never ratified by Congress, but it served to keep the Indians quiet for a time.[7]

General Garland, not satisfied that the Mescaleros had been sufficiently punished, contented himself with establishing a fort in the heart of Mescalero country. Miles' force had been assembled for the purpose of engaging in operations against the Mescalero Apaches, and Camp Stanton was well placed for that campaign. But the location lacked many of the essentials for an effective garrison. On April 18, 1855, Miles advised Garland that no wood for building was available, only brush and scraggly little trees, and further that, within fifteen miles of

4

the camp, grass was poor and scarce. Major Carleton and his guides suggested that the post be located at a point some fifteen or twenty miles further up in the mountains. Grass was much better at the suggested location and building timber was plentiful. Miles decided to investigate personally, advising Garland that if a more suitable location was found, he would move immediately and start building the new post.[8]

First Miles investigated the country around the Ruidoso River, concluding that the grass was insufficient to support his animals, nor was there enough wood for a sizable command. He also felt that placing a fort in the Ruidoso area would put it too far east to be effective in controlling the Mescaleros. On April 21, Miles left Camp Stanton with two companies, one of cavalry and one of infantry, and marched fifteen miles to a camp established by Major Carleton. This camp, which Carleton named "Camp Garland" in honor of General Garland, rested on the site Carleton had recommended as most suitable for a garrison.[9]

Camp Garland was located on the Rio Hondo, formed by the junction of the Ruidoso and Bonito Rivers, a short distance downstream from the Bonito River. This was an ideal spot to monitor Apache movements, regardless of what direction they chose to travel. Miles found ample water, grass, firewood, and building timber readily available at that site.[10] In fact, the region contained a plethora of rich soil, lush grasses, water, game, and fish. The area also enjoyed ample rainfall and a mild climate. Colonel Miles reported that the region, with an abundance of ideal farmland, was capable of supporting a vast population.[11] By April 28 Miles had moved his entire command to Camp Garland. Before beginning construction of the fort, Miles decided to establish security for the camp and those building the fort. He initiated construction of two block houses and defensive works for one company on April 29. These were intended for defense of the camp and were not part of the fort.[12]

Miles' orders were specific, he was to build the fort on the Bonito River. In his report of April 28, Miles proposed the revised site and requested permission from Garland to locate the fort on the Hondo.[13] Knowing that General Garland was *en route* to visit the camp when he wrote the report, Miles included directions on how to reach Camp Garland in his dispatch. When General Garland arrived at Miles' camp early in May, he overruled Miles' choice of site and elected to stay with

5

his original decision to establish the new fort on the Bonito. On May 4, 1855, General Garland issued orders officially establishing the fort 156 miles southeast of Albuquerque on the Rio Bonito.[14] Pvt James A. Bennett, 1st Dragoons, recorded in his diary that when Garland selected the site for the new fort, the officers all got drunk![15] Apparently a final decision was cause for celebration. Pending Department of the Army approval, Garland temporarily named the fort after Captain Stanton and was pleased when higher authority did not change the name.[16]

The new four-company post was situated approximately twenty miles upstream from the junction of the Rio Bonito with the Rio Ruidoso. It would be fifteen miles south of Capitan Mountain, twenty miles northeast of *Sierra Blanca*, and over 100 miles from its nearest military neighbor, Fort Craig. The nearest post office was Albuquerque. The Surgeon General reported the exact location of the fort as 33° 29' 27" north latitude and 105° 28' 19" west longitude.[17] Fort Stanton's exact distance from Albuquerque and Fort Fillmore remained something of a controversy for some time. The post returns for May stated that the fort was 156 miles from Albuquerque. However, Lt. John W. Davidson, who commanded Stanton's company briefly following his death, had made the trip from Albuquerque to Fort Stanton several times and claimed that Albuquerque was 178 miles distant. Miles believed the distance to Fort Fillmore to be 160 miles, but his officers all agreed that his estimate was at least twenty miles short. According to these estimates, Fort Fillmore was farther away than Albuquerque. Other sources place Albuquerque at distances ranging from 150 to 275 miles, depending upon the route chosen and the hardships the traveler was willing to endure.[18]

The garrison of Fort Stanton, as of the end of May 1855, consisted of:

    Companies I and K, 1st Dragoons
    Companies A and K, 3rd Infantry
    Company B, 8th Infantry
    Company C, New Mexico Volunteers
with detachments from:
    Companies C and E, 3rd Infantry
    Companies E, I, and K, 8th Infantry
In addition, the Department of New Mexico assigned one Assistant

Surgeon to the post, for an aggregate of 412 officers and men. The entire garrison, except for Company A, 3rd Infantry, had transferred to the post on May 4 from Camp Garland. Company A transferred to Fort Stanton on May 31, from Fort Fillmore. On May 5, 1855, Department Order 9 placed Capt. Bvt. Ltc. Isaac V. D. Reeve, 8th Infantry, in command of the newly established fort and directed that Colonel Miles return to Fort Fillmore.[19]

The establishment of Fort Stanton and the presence of a garrison fostered immigration to the region. The United States Census of 1850 listed the Anglo population of New Mexico Territory as 1,600, of which just under 1,000 were Army personnel. This figure included personnel stationed at El Paso and San Elizario, even though they were actually outside the territory. The rest of the population of New Mexico Territory was Indian or Hispanic and had lived in New Mexico since before the Mexican War.[20] Fort Stanton was built near a small group of Hispanic villages known as Las Placitas de Los Rio Bonito or Las Placitas. The 1850 census did not list these communities and information on the area for that period is sketchy. The largest of these villages, about nine miles from Fort Stanton as the crow flies, was known variously as La Placita de Los Rio Bonito, La Placita, or Bonito Plaza. This community, renamed Lincoln in 1869, was listed on the 1860 census as Rio Bonito.[21]

Even before work began on the new fort, people learned of General Garland's plans to build a fort in the region and announced their intentions to establish farms in the area. Following the establishment of Fort Stanton, the population of the region grew rapidly. The 1860 census of Socorro County listed 257 residents of Rio Bonito, including thirty-six families. Most of the residents were Hispanic, but seventy-eight people (30%), including thirteen families, were from the United States, Canada, and Europe. More than sixty percent of the non-Hispanic residents had emigrated from the United States and eight Anglo children had been born in Rio Bonito. Real estate holdings were valued at $25,775 and personal wealth at $50,813. Nearly all of these holdings were in small ranches and farms. Of twenty-three farmers residing in Rio Bonito, only six were Hispanic while thirty-six of the forty-five laborers were Hispanic. All of the Hispanic farmers were relatively

7

wealthy while the laborers, with few exceptions, had no assets. The census of Rio Bonito catalogued a wide variety of occupations, including one musician (aged sixty), two teamsters, two carpenters, a blacksmith, two millers, eight herders, and a variety of others.[22] Socorro County, established in 1852, between Valencia and Doña Ana Counties, included Fort Stanton and the Peñasco, Ruidoso, Bonito, and Hondo River valleys. The 1860 census for Socorro County enumerated 1,381 dwelling houses, 1217 families, and a population the size of New Mexico's entire 1850 population.[23]

Although Fort Stanton was in a remote area, the region was bountiful and would invite settlement once the fort provided protection. However, building the fort was not an easy task. All of the soldiers at Camp Garland, except the volunteers, worked to gather materials from the surrounding area and build the fort. The volunteers' contract excluded them from manual labor.[24]

Conditions were less than ideal and not everything went smoothly. Shortages of tradesmen, work animals, tools, supplies (including paper and blank forms), and experienced officers created problems. The nearest supply depot was at Albuquerque and poor roads made re-supply very difficult. The roads built by Carleton's and Miles' columns in March were sufficient to serve a force in the field for a few weeks, but soon proved woefully inadequate for a four-company post.

Upon his return to Fort Fillmore, Miles wrote to Reeve pointing out that the roads were not suited for wagons. In response, 2nd. Lt. Silas P. Higgins reconnoitered a possible road from Fort Stanton to the junction of the Ruidoso and Carrizo rivers and reported that only a few hours work was required to construct the road. Relieved by Company A, 3rd Infantry, Company K, 3rd Infantry departed Fort Stanton on June 2, and Reeve directed the company commander, 2nd Lt. Lawrence W. O'Bannon, to open this road on the way out.[25]

All supplies for the Army in New Mexico Territory came to Fort Union via the Santa Fe trail and were distributed from there to other posts in the territory. Routes to Albuquerque, Santa Fe and points south from Fort Union went by way of Anton Chico, a junction point for trade routes in New Mexico. From Anton Chico a road ran along the west bank of the Pecos River through Albuquerque, and as far south as

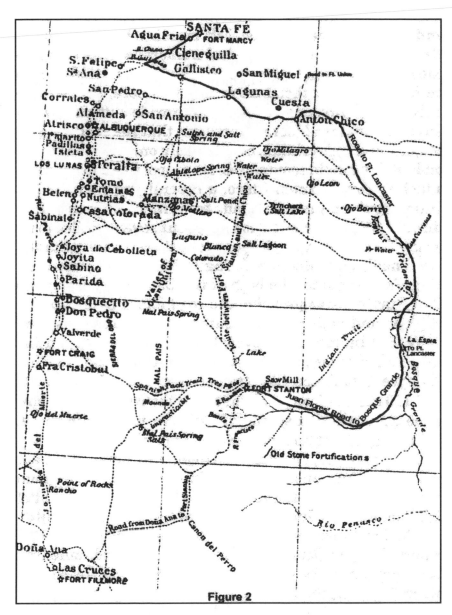

Figure 2

First road built for communication between Fort Stanton and supply depots at Santa Fe and Fort Union. This road, scouted by Juan Flores, joined the Fort Lancaster Road near Bosque Grande. The distance to Anton Chico from Fort Stanton on this route was 275 miles. (adapted from the atlas to accompany *The Official Records of the Union and Confederate Armies, 1861–1865*, Part I, plate 54, map 1).

9

Fort Lancaster in Texas. A link with this road was vital to Fort Stanton. Juan Flores, a civilian guide at the fort, indicated he could find a good road for wagons around the east end of the Capitans to Bosque Grande, a watering place on the Anton Chico–Fort Lancaster road. Flores set out on June 2 to search for water along his intended route. Reeve planned to have Lieutenant Higgins set out a track for wagons if Flores found water. Although Higgins had been on several expeditions in the area, he had made no maps for lack of paper.[26]

In early June, Lt. Isaac J. Moore, of the 1st Dragoons stationed at Los Lunas, reported that the road from Anton Chico to Fort Stanton was about 275 miles long and would require a great deal of labor and expense to make it serviceable. He cited the principal problems with the road as: (a) sand from Agua Negra to the lower end of the Bosque Redondo, (b) salt marshes between Bosque Grande and the Rio Bonito, and (c) numerous cliffs along the Rio Bonito requiring bridges where no timber was available to build them. According to Moore, this road could provide water for draft animals, but in some places it could supply only about fifty animals. He proposed a shorter route—from Anton Chico, a central point on the Fort Union–Albuquerque road, to Trinchera Mesa, then through an uncharted region for about 70 miles to the base of the Sierra Capitans. From there to Fort Stanton he estimated was one day's march. This last leg of Moore's route, from the base of the Capitan Mountains to Fort Stanton, was probably the road found by Lieutenant Higgins and improved by Lieutenant O'Bannon's K Company, 3rd Infantry. However, Moore did not mention this road in his report. The new route would reduce the traveling distance from Anton Chico to Fort Stanton to between 150 and 160 miles. Moore's letters explained that the region would have to be explored by a specially equipped party with picked animals and that no guides were available to help.[27]

In September, Lieutenant Higgins explored the Capitans searching unsuccessfully for a new road, but found that a road through the gorge was not feasible. Also in September, General Garland sent Lieutenant Moore to explore the area he had described in his June letters. Early in October, Moore reported his discovery of a good route from Los Lunas and Anton Chico to Fort Stanton. In spite of Moore's finding, the Army did not build a new wagon road until 1857. The new road ran from

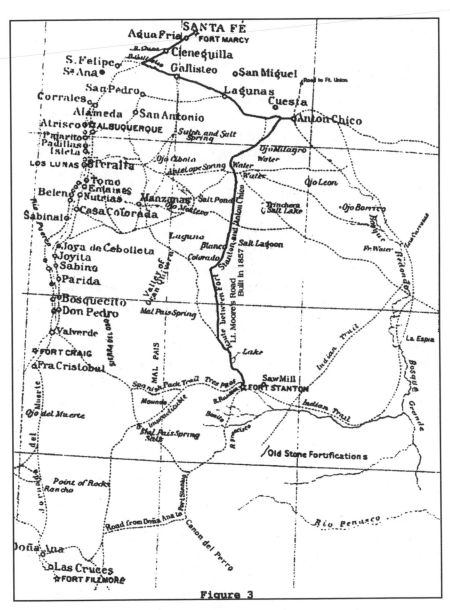

Figure 3

Road built in 1857 as a result of Lieutenant Moore's scout. This road reduced the travel distance to Anton Chico by approximately 125 miles and substantially reduced travel time and shipping costs to Fort Stanton from Fort Union and Santa Fe. (Adapted from the *Atlas to Accompany the Official Records of the Union and Confederate Armies, 1861–1865*: Part I, plate 54, map 1)

Fort Stanton to the base of the Capitan Mountains and from there directly to Anton Chico, where it joined the Fort Union to Albuquerque road. This route substantially reduced the cost, in both time and money, of transportation to Fort Stanton.[28] It came too late, however, to help the construction crew with its logistics problems.

Problems caused by lack of tools and qualified personnel were as vexing as the problems caused by poor roads. Unhappy with the progress being made, Reeve wrote to the Acting Assistant Adjutant General (AAAG), in mid-June 1855, presenting a list of personnel deficiencies at the fort that were hampering construction efforts. Reeve explained that he needed experienced master carpenters, master masons, and "a competent blacksmith, if one can be found in the command."[29] He stressed that construction of Fort Stanton was currently being accomplished, from necessity, entirely by soldiers not qualified for the job. Citing the importance of the fort and its location, Reeve pointed out that work was progressing very slowly and it would ultimately save time and money to have competent foremen supervising the work. At the top of Reeve's list was the need for an experienced quartermaster. Reeve emphasized that he found no fault with his present quartermaster, but that the young man was inexperienced and over-worked. The Acting Adjutant for Quartermaster (AAQM) was Bvt. 2nd Lt. Richard V. Boumeau, 3rd Infantry. Boumeau was also Acting Adjutant for Commissary Stores (AACS) and Post Adjutant.[30]

In early July, Reeve explained to General Garland that, barring interruptions, the troops would be comfortably housed for the winter, provided the sawmill promised earlier by the Quartermaster in Santa Fe arrived in time. The foundation for the first permanent building, the commissary storeroom, was nearly ready for the men to start laying adobes. However, the adobe makers, Hispanic civilians brought from Albuquerque, could not produce a sufficient number of adobes per day. The number of draft animals available was also inadequate. Adding to the problem, the animals on hand could not be worked every day because Headquarters provided only quarter rations for them. Grazing could not supplement the animals' feed, as might be expected, because the animals had to be penned at night for security and the grass was poor due to a drought. Therefore it was necessary to allot half the workdays for the animals to graze. Reeve respectfully brought this to the general's attention because the quartermaster at Headquarters had thus far failed to address the problem. He stressed that work would be seriously hampered if the garrison was not soon supplied with more animals or plenty of corn for the ones on hand.[31]

By mid-July Reeve was becoming exasperated. On July 15, Reeve wrote a terse note to Headquarters complaining that he had no blank post returns. In fact, he complained, no blank forms of any kind were on hand for post use. In another letter, written the same day, Reeve explained that he did not have enough mechanics of any kind, especially carpenters, masons and blacksmiths. He again wrote that the one blacksmith at the post was not competent to do the work required of him, even if he had the help of a good striker, which he did not. Reeve brought to the attention of the commanding general the fact that his AACS had requested commissary stores from Headquarters in May and emphasized the need for an immediate response. As of July 15 the fort had only twenty days' provisions, and Headquarters had not yet acknowledged the AACS' request.[32]

About mid July, Reeve became convinced that the material in the adobes was too brittle. He decided that stone would be more satisfactory and put the adobe makers to work quarrying stone. Later in July, Colonel Reeve received orders transferring him to Fort Bliss to command that post and almost simultaneously was ordered to Fort Bliss immediately to testify before a court-martial. Before he left Fort Stanton, Reeve sent the adobe makers back to Albuquerque. Reeve was relieved by Bvt. Maj. Jefferson Van Horne, who arrived at Fort Stanton on August 2, 1855. On his way to the post, Van Horne encountered the adobe makers, en route to Albuquerque, but upon arrival found no record of why Reeve had sent them away. The post adjutant told him that Reeve, with permission from Headquarters, intended to make the buildings of stone. Since no record of this permission existed, Van Horne requested General Garland's approval before proceeding with stone. An ample supply of adobes was on hand for the hospital and commissary storeroom, and Van Horne directed that they be completed with adobe while awaiting Garland's response. The hospital and commissary storeroom became the first two permanent buildings completed at Fort Stanton.[33]

Major Van Horne inherited a deteriorating situation at Fort Stanton. When he arrived the post was out of subsistence stores and the command was on short rations. The only subsistence available was what had arrived with Van Horne and his twenty-man escort. A shipment of cattle was past due and Lieutenant Higgins, accompanied by a small detachment, was out looking for it. Company A, 3rd Infantry was scheduled to be sent to Albuquerque for discharge, and the company was widely scattered, including both the detachment escorting Reeve to Fort Bliss and the one with Higgins looking for the shipment of beef.[34] Trying to assess the situation, Reeve inquired as to whether the New Mexico Volunteers were to muster out at the fort or travel elsewhere. He reported that if the volunteers were to extend, he needed mounts for them because theirs were jaded due to lack of rations and poor grass. Reeve received orders that the volunteers were to immediately travel to Albuquerque for discharge. Having judged their animals unserviceable, Reeve lent mules to the volunteers and dispatched them to Albuquerque, leaving the post with few work animals.

In a report dated August 19, Van Horne emphasized that the mules taken by the New Mexico Volunteers had not yet been returned and were desperately needed. He also requested three yoke of oxen, because oxen were better suited to hauling timber. When Company A departed the post, Van Horne retained Pvt. Leonard Patrick, a saddler whose services were sorely needed. However, on October 25, Headquarters issued Special Order 103 ordering Patrick to join his company.[35]

Skilled labor and draft animals were not the only items in short supply. Van Horne soon learned that the tools on hand were badly worn and insufficient in number. Spades, shovels, masons' trowels, and whipsaws were badly needed. The troops had no half-round files with which to sharpen the saws. The man employed in the smithy was not a blacksmith and knew very little about such work. The farrier for Company B, 1st Dragoons, did all of the shoeing. Windows and doors for the hospital and commissary storeroom had not yet arrived. On August 5, Van Horne offered to send a detail to pick up the doors and windows as well as some badly needed carpenter's tools.[36]

When the promised sawmill arrived, near the end of August, it proved to be defective. Parts were missing and others were duplicated. A civilian employee at the fort, one Mr. Jones, commented that it was

Typical officer's quarters at Fort Stanton. A curtain obscures the window by which the chair is sitting. Larger rooms were unnecessary because the men spent little time in them. Fort Stanton, Inc. maintains a small museum for the public at the fort. In it are preserved several rooms and many artifacts. *Photo courtesy of the author*

the poorest sawmill he had ever seen. After a week of finding parts and making repairs, the sawmill was put into operation on September 5, and it did facilitate the building effort.[37] With the sawmill working, the need for draft animals to haul timber intensified. Van Horne eased the problem somewhat by having the troops make yokes and use the cattle from the post's beef herd to haul logs. By September 10, Van Horne was pleased with the production of the sawmill.[38]

No sooner was the sawmill put into operation than the limekiln, built in May, failed. Van Horne had another kiln built but was not happy with the quality of the lime he was getting. The limestone was of poor quality and produced lime "more the quality of chalk."[39] Nor was the local sand satisfactory for making mortar and Van Horne found suitable sand difficult to locate.[40] Van Horne eventually located satisfactory limestone, because on September 21 he reported the limekiln was producing excellent lime.[41]

A view of the stables as they appear today. The original adobe part of the structure is behind this building. The silo was added in the late 1880s. *Photo courtesy of the author*

By Early September, the troops were putting the final touches on the commissary storeroom and hospital, and laying foundations for three sets of company quarters and corresponding officers quarters. In the absence of a reply from General Garland to his inquiry of August 4 regarding the use of stone, Van Horne proceeded with stone instead of adobe. By the end of September, most of the more serious problems had been solved. Problems of a nuisance variety persisted, however. On October 30, Van Horne received, in response to an earlier request, a letter informing him that headquarters had no blank post returns either. In November, Van Horne requested a copy of the plans for the fort from Santa Fe because his copy was inaccurate and ragged.[42]

Sgt. James A. Bennett, 1st Dragoons, arrived at Fort Stanton in mid-August 1855 and recorded his impressions in his diary.[43] His entry for August 13 states that the post had quarters for eight officers and one company. Bennett noted the post also sported commissary and quartermaster storerooms and a guardhouse. He observed that all the soldiers were busily at work, presumably on construction of the fort.[44]

The buildings of the finished fort were made mostly of materials available in the immediate vicinity, ribble stone and adobe. The roofs were shingled and the barracks floors were earth.[45] This type of construction, dirt floors not withstanding, made the fort more durable and more comfortable than most of the posts in the territory.[46]

The 1870 Surgeon General's Report indicates that Fort Stanton was built on the south bank of the Rio Bonito, seventy-five feet above the stream bed, and was laid out in rectangular form with one side paralleling the river. According to the report, the original configuration was as follows: The commanding officer's quarters were located near the center of the side of the parade ground adjacent to the river. On the opposite side stood a building containing the adjutant's office, guardroom, and a detention cell. This building was flanked by two sets of company quarters. One set of company quarters, a storehouse and one building designed to house four sets of officers' quarters faced each of the remaining sides of the parade ground. The buildings were heated by fireplaces and ventilated by chimneys, cupolas, and windows.[47] In 1859, Quartermaster General Col. Joseph E. Johnston, touring the Southwest on an inspection tour, reported that Fort Stanton was the only post he had seen in the department that had a semblance of durability.[48]

The guardhouse, made of adobe, was obviously not as durable as Johnston might have expected; because on September 19, 1855, two men escaped by digging a hole through the wall. Sergeant Bennett, with four men, went in pursuit of the escapees but never caught them. While Bennett was pursuing the fugitives his company left the post on a scout. When his company returned, the sergeant was court-martialed for being absent without leave. Fortunately, he was acquitted of the charges.[49] Despite the flawed guardhouse, the post was one of the most sturdy in the Department, and water was easily obtained without digging wells.

The Rio Bonito provided water for the fort's needs. While it remains a puzzle just how water was supplied to various points within the post prior to 1869, the system was probably little different from that described in the Surgeon General's Report for 1870. Water entered the fort by way of an aqueduct three quarters of a mile long running from the river to the southwest corner of the parade ground. From there an *acequia,* or ditch, surrounded the parade ground about twenty feet in front of the barracks and officers' quarters. In 1869, or early 1870, the officers planted trees around the parade ground and dug the *ace-*

quia to irrigate the trees.[50] Upon exiting the *acequia* the water passed by the hospital via a single aqueduct and exited the post by way of the corrals, flowing into the river again. Sinks were dug behind each set of barracks and quarters and privies were constructed, at a distance, flanking the officers' quarters. An adobe sink was located behind the hospital with water drainage and urinals behind the sink. The slope of the terrain provided natural drainage. This system had its advantages, but the fort's dependence upon the river for water occasionally caused problems. During times when the Rio Bonito was very low, the post garden could not be irrigated and drinking water was scarce, leading to health problems.[51]

In September 1857, Capt. John N. Macomb of the Topographical Engineers proposed that the Fort Stanton reservation be an area twelve miles square, centered on the parade ground and oriented north-south and east-west, relative to true north. On May 12, 1859, President James Buchanan officially established this reservation by Executive Order. Covering 144 square miles, Fort Stanton Military Reservation was the largest in New Mexico Territory.[52] This reserve also had the distinction of being one of only a few in the territory that did not infringe on the rights of private property. Other forts, such as Fort Union and Fort Craig, were on land belonging to individuals or corporations.[53]

Although the government claimed 144 square miles, the region surrounding Fort Stanton offered an abundance of rich land available for farmers and ranchers. People began settling in the valleys of the Bonito and Ruidoso rivers and particularly in the immediate vicinity of Fort Stanton, where protection from Indian depredations would be most effective. Among the early arrivals were General Garland's son David, a civilian, and one A. M. Clenny, who came to the area in 1855. Garland became the first postmaster at Fort Stanton, and Clenny established a farm where he lived until his death in 1898. A small group of farmers settled at Patos Spring, eighteen miles from the fort, and planted a large corn crop. In February 1857 three men, claiming to represent a group of forty farmers, came to the post to request protection from Indian raids. By 1860 thirty-six families had settled near Fort Stanton and numerous farms and ranches were widely dispersed in the nearby valleys. Indicative of a thriving community, a wide representa-

18

tion of the trades was present, including seamstress, miller, teamster, musician, cook, carpenter and blacksmith.[54]

The presence of a large, widely dispersed, community within the aegis of the fort taxed the garrison's ability to provide effective protection. In fact, the troops of Fort Stanton were heavily engaged fighting Indians even before the first blockhouses at the camp were finished. While the troops were fully occupied in the construction effort, the Indians raided the Army herds. Mule meat was a delicacy to the Indians, so they stole horses and mules, riding the horses and eating the mules.[55] The easy pickings provided good times for the Mescalero Apaches, and the Capitan, Sacramento, Organ, and Jicarilla Mountains provided good hiding places. One of the Indians' favorite tricks was to leave a clear trail, leading the pursuing scout around until their horses were exhausted. Then they would attack, provided the soldiers were not well armed or too numerous. In this way the Indians acquired horses, weapons, ammunition and the leather from the saddles and paraphernalia.[56]

In early June 1855, a party of Indians wore out the horses and men of two detachments from Fort Stanton. The guide, Juan Flores, discovered the party's tracks in a gorge approaching the Bonito River about eighteen miles from the post on June 8 or 9. The following Sunday morning, June 10, Ltc. Isaac V. D. Reeve, commanding the post, dispatched two details to pursue this band of Indians. One detail of ninety men, composed of detachments from two companies with Flores as guide and commanded by Bvt. Maj. William N. Grier, traveled along the Bonito River. Colonel Reeve wanted to avoid trouble with the Mescaleros pending an upcoming council between them and the Governor. In order to avoid the appearance of infidelity to the agreement, Reeve ordered Grier not to pursue the Indians if they entered Mescalero country. The second detail, a company of mounted volunteers commanded by Capt. Miguel E. Pina, scouted the gorge where Juan Flores had discovered the tracks.[57]

The Indians noticed the two search parties quickly and fled toward the Chameleon Mountains. Captain Pina's detail found their trail early Monday morning, June 11, and immediately gave chase. At the start, the pack mules were unable to keep up and Pina left them behind in a

19

ciénaga, or marshy watering spot, on the trail. By Tuesday evening fatigue and lack of water had taken its toll and the horses in Pina's command were exhausted; two of them died. The troops had not eaten since leaving the pack mules on Monday morning and were as jaded as the horses. At five o'clock Tuesday evening Pina, forced to give up the chase, turned toward the *ciénaga* and his mules.[58]

Major Grier first went along the Bonito River to determine if the Indians had crossed and were headed into Mescalero country. After satisfying himself that they had not crossed the Bonito, Grier marched around the east end of the Capitans to try to pick up the trail. He found the trail Monday afternoon but left it late that evening to find water and camp. Tuesday morning Grier recovered the trail and determined that it was a large party and that Pina's volunteers were in hot pursuit. That evening about ten o'clock he camped at the *ciénaga* where Pina left his mules.[59]

The next morning, Wednesday, June 13, Grier's party marched only about a half mile before they encountered two of Pina's men, exhausted, famished, and thirsty. Grier immediately returned to his last night's camp and sent water to Pina. At five o'clock that afternoon Pina's bedraggled command arrived at Grier's camp with most of the men on foot. Grier sent for fresh mounts for twenty of Pina's men and five days' supplies, which arrived the next day. Pina sent half of his men back to Fort Stanton with the broken-down animals while he and Grier took the rest of the troops and returned to the pursuit. They followed the Indians' trail to the Gallinas and Chameleon Mountains before giving up the chase. The detachment arrived back at Fort Stanton on the morning of June 20, with exhausted animals.[60]

Just before giving up the chase, Pina had come within sight of the band he was pursuing. He saw only a few Indians but judged from the number of tracks that the raiding party numbered about fifty, half on horseback and half on foot, with many animals. The Indians had been crafty, and Pina believed they knew where to obtain just enough water for themselves. Whether planned that way by the raiders or not, Pina's men were unable to obtain water at the watering places after the Indians had been there. The fugitives had taken a circuitous route and chosen rough terrain. The pursuit from the *ciénaga* had taken over seventy-five miles, while the return trip took only thirty-five.[61] The effort

20

was not entirely fruitless, however. Pina forced the fleeing band to abandon two mules, four horses, meat, buffalo hides, and blankets. A small boy, two or three years old, was also abandoned and taken back to the fort by Pina.[62]

Grier learned that the raiders were a band of Jicarilla Apaches and believed them to have been driven from Raton and Mesa Rico by a force of New Mexico Volunteers. The New Mexico Volunteers were punishing the Ute and Jicarilla Apache Indians throughout their homelands. These Hispanic troops performed most creditably and, according to Robert Utley, "...dramatically disproved the common Anglo charge that they would not fight."[63] A large number of Jicarilla Apaches were moving into Mescalero country and Reeve believed they came seeking sanctuary, unaware of the presence of U.S. troops.[64] By August the garrison at Fort Stanton barely had the resources to meet the demands placed upon it.

On the morning of August 22, 1855, Van Horne, commanding the post, received orders to send a detachment to establish communication with Capt. John Pope, Topographical Engineers. Pope, digging artesian wells on the *Llano Estacado*, or Staked Plains, near the Pecos River in Texas, had reported losing seven men in an attack by Comanche Indians. Van Horne did not have sufficient troops to comply until Capt. John W. Davidson, Company B, 1st Dragoons, returned that afternoon with a detail escorting a train.[65] Van Horne ordered Davidson to depart on the mission immediately. Davidson distrusted the Mescalero Apaches and believed they were responsible for recent outrages near El Paso. Arguing that he would need the full strength of his company, Davidson asked permission to wait for ten of his men to return from escort duty. Van Horne reluctantly agreed, but Davidson was to leave by the 27th, whether his men arrived or not. Davidson's men never made it back and he delayed until August 28 before leaving. Davidson took thirty-five men from Company B, the guide Juan Flores, a howitzer for extra protection against Indian attack, and twenty mules. Much to Van Horn's consternation, Davidson took so many men and animals that he left the garrison short handed and without enough mules to provide mounted protection for the work details.[66]

Despite the shortage of personnel, the troops at Fort Stanton maintained the peace so effectively that the War Department decided the

21

garrison could safely be reduced. In May 1855, the Mescalero Apaches signed a treaty with Governor Meriwether and, although they were responsible for a few incidents, remained fairly peaceful until the advent of the Civil War.[67] In the Spring of 1857 the Army, satisfied that the area surrounding the Bonito, Ruidoso and Peñasco rivers was peaceful, decided to move two companies from Fort Stanton to duty elsewhere. On April 12, Maj. Theophilus H. Holmes, commander at Fort Stanton, wrote to headquarters in Santa Fe protesting the move. He explained that the local Indians were quiet at present but it was an enforced quietude. Major Holmes pointed out that the removal of a large number of troops from the fort would weaken it to the point that it would be in a purely defensive position. This would be too much of a temptation for the Indians, who would take advantage of the situation to perpetrate depredations. If they did, the situation would be unten-able for settlers in the neighborhood.[68]

Holmes' protests apparently made an impression. That same month General Garland informed Holmes that Fort Stanton would remain a four-company post. Garland noted his decision on the jacket of Holmes' April 12 letter and directed that Company E, Independent Regiment of Mounted Rifles (RMR), which had already moved, was to be considered on detached service. However, this did not alleviate Holmes' immediate problems. Company D, 2nd Artillery, with ten pri-vates from Company K, 8th Infantry, was on a protracted scout pursu-ant to Department orders and Company E, RMR, was in Santa Fe on detached service. This left the post with less than two full companies of Infantry. Post returns listed only five officers on duty at the post, including the assistant surgeon.[69] Nevertheless, at least officially, Fort Stanton remained a four-company post, but only for a time.

Department Order 15, dated January 25, 1859, transferred Company B, RMR, from Fort Stanton. Because Company B needed time to repair wagons, shoe mules, and make other preparations, the com-pany did not leave Fort Stanton until February 28. From the time Company B left the fort until June 1860, Fort Stanton was assigned only three companies. At about the same time Company B was transferred, a rumor circulated that the garrison was to be reduced to two infantry companies. A group of citizens, residing variously from twelve to 211 miles from the fort, presented a petition to the post commander to be forwarded to Department Headquarters. The petition, signed by twenty-four Anglos and seven Hispanics, pointed out that a significant number of American settlers lived in the area. It stated that since, in the event of an Indian attack, pursuit must be immediate and fast, cavalry was necessary. The petition stressed that the terrain and conditions in the region rendered infantry almost useless against Indians. The citizens wanted at least two companies of cavalry at the fort. The post commander, Maj. Charles F. Ruff, added his endorsement to the bottom of the petition as if it were a postscript, before forwarding the petition, without introduction, to Col. Benjamin L. E. Bonneville, the Department commander. Ruff noted in his endorsement that the presence of a large military force was all that kept the Indians peaceful, the same argument Maj. Theophilus H. Holmes had used in 1857. Ruff signed both the petition and his postscript.[70]

The effect the petition had is unclear. Although most of the troops remaining at the post were cavalry, the size of the garrison was reduced. In June 1860, Company K, 8th Infantry, moved to Fort Union, leaving the post with only two companies until August, when Company I, 8th Infantry joined the garrison. The aggregate number of personnel at Fort Stanton remained around 230 from February 1859 until June 1860, as compared to about 415 from May 1855 to April 1857.[71] The citizens living in the region wanted a larger garrison, but they had other reasons, in addition to protection, for wanting a large garrison at Fort Stanton. They lived in an isolated area and needed a market for their goods.

Fort Stanton was a hundred miles from its nearest neighbor and nearly twice that distance from its primary supply depot in Albuquerque. All supplies had to be brought in over rough roads, each of which crossed at least one mountain range and had some very difficult sections. The 275 miles from the junction at Anton Chico to Fort Stanton was impractical for wagons because it was a narrow road over mountainous terrain and lacked sufficient water for draft animals. Goods had to travel an even longer route, going first to Fort Fillmore, 180 miles from Fort Stanton. Transportation costs made everything delivered under contract to Fort Stanton more expensive than at nearly any other post in New Mexico. In 1857, a good road was built which joined the Fort Union–Albuquerque road near Anton Chico and reduced the traveling distance from Anton Chico to Fort Stanton by about 115 miles. The new road reduced the cost of goods delivered under contract, but goods were still expensive and the Army wanted to reduce costs.[72]

For the farmers and ranchers around Fort Stanton, transporting produce to market centers such as Albuquerque, Mesilla or El Paso was a daunting task. However, the post provided a profitable market and local farmers and ranchers could supply the post much more cheaply than anyone else. By 1858, locally grown corn and hay satisfied Fort Stanton's requirements. Farms in the area produced about 12,000 bushels of corn as well as wheat and oats. Bvt. Ltc. John B. Grayson, Assistant Adjutant of Commissary and Subsistence, authorized Colonel Reeve, post commander, to purchase six months' supply of fodder starting December 1, 1858. The post commissary officer purchased 420 *fanegas* of corn at $3.00 per *fanega* and 980 *fanegas* of corn at $2.75 each. One *fanega* equals two and a half bushels, or approximately 140 pounds.[73] He also purchased 100 tons of fodder at $20.00 per ton, putting almost $6,000 into the local economy.[74] The feed was intended for the beef cattle herd at the fort and cost considerably less than the corn and hay purchased under contract for the fort in the same year by the Quartermaster Department.[75]

By 1859, Army officials believed that in years of normal rainfall and good crops, enough corn would be grown near Fort Stanton to fulfill its needs and an ample supply of excellent hay could be cut.[76] Irish potatoes, valued by the Army as an antiscorbutic, were grown in New Mexico for the first time in 1859. That year the farmers around Rio Bonito harvested Irish potatoes, apparently for sale to Fort Stanton. Col. Benjamin L. E. Bonneville visited the region in June. He enthusiastically predicted good crops of various grains, including 12,000 bushels of corn. Bonneville had not taken nature into account. A drought began in 1859 that seriously reduced harvests. Area farmers produced only 8,850 bushels of corn. The crops of wheat and beans were also poor and local farmers harvested only 706 bushels of potatoes.[77]

Throughout the Department of New Mexico agricultural production for 1860 was estimated to be 25–50 percent less per acre than in

24

years of normal rainfall. Despite the drought, crops increased substantially, especially in those items purchased by the Army.[78] A symbiotic relationship existed between the farmers and ranchers, who provided inexpensive commissary and subsistence stores, and the fort, which provided protection and kept the peace. For some, however, the post was not the only customer, nor even the main customer. Trade in whisky, arms, and ammunition threatened the tenuous peace of the region.

Unscrupulous traders along the Bonito, Peñasco, Sapello, Felix and lower Rio Grande sold whiskey, fresh horses and the latest firearms to the Indians. Deserters also contributed to the problem by selling their horses, weapons and ammunition to the Indians for "traveling money."[79] In September 1859, Major Ruff apparently tried to curb the trade in arms and ammunition. He wrote to Headquarters asking if any law, regulation, or Department order existed prohibiting the sale of either arms, ammunition, or both to Indians. If so, he requested that he be furnished a copy. Lt. John D. Wilkins, Acting Assistant Adjutant General for the Department of New Mexico, investigated the matter and learned that no such law existed for the department. The Mescaleros were peaceful at the time and no further reference to the subject appeared in post returns or correspondence.[80]

The most exasperating problem for post commanders was the sale of whiskey to Indians and soldiers. In the fall of 1855, the sutler's clerk at Fort Stanton complained to the Indian Agent that settlers along the Bonito River were being bothered a great deal by drunken Indians. In 1856, David Garland had several altercations with a man named Clenny over whiskey. Garland accused Clenny of making whiskey and selling it to the Indians.[81] The Indians had serious problems with alcohol. Letters of the time report that drinking at one Indian gathering resulted in fights that killed six of their own people.[82]

The situation did not improve over time and, in 1859 Capt. Thomas Claiborne, post commander, complained bitterly that the whiskey sellers along the Bonito River were creating serious problems. He was upset about Mexicans coming up from Durango to the post and the Hispanic communities along the Rio Bonito, and selling whiskey. Claiborne was particularly annoyed by the community of La Placita

(Lincoln). In La Placita whiskey sellers, as many as sixty or more at a time, openly sold whiskey to Indians. Claiborne complained that whiskey vendors, which included nearly everyone, sold freely to the Indians, then, when things got out of hand, came running to the fort for protection.[83]

Claiborne became especially aggravated with a Mr. Hacket, the proprietor of a "hog ranch" near the fort. Hog ranches were low-grade drinking establishments, which typically also provided gambling and prostitution. Enterprises such as Hacket's usually occupied a tent, or similar make-shift arrangement which provided a modicum of shelter and was portable.[84] On November 7, Claiborne sent an officer to bring in absentees from Hacket's "ranch" and tell Hacket to leave. Hacket was selling whisky to the Mescaleros and would not leave. Five days later, before breakfast, Hacket came to Fort Stanton and asked Claiborne to provide him with guards because the Indians had become unruly. Claiborne told Hacket to get out. That evening Hacket came back wanting a guard and escort. He was being harassed by the Indians and was afraid they would destroy his property. Claiborne remarked that he was glad of it and hoped the Indians would leave no vestige of Hacket's enterprise. In a letter to Headquarters on November 16, Claiborne explained that he had spoken with Cadette and other Mescalero chiefs and found them very much disposed toward peace, but the whiskey trade was making it difficult for them to control their young men. Claiborne felt that it would be folly to allow whisky venders to provoke a war and wanted to be rid of them.[85] A common desire for peace was apparent.

The peace with the Mescaleros was fragile, and whiskey was not the only irritant. The Indians were prone to stealing livestock. Usually they traveled to Mexico, stealing horses and mules and bringing them back across the border.[86] The commanders at Fort Stanton tended to ignore this activity but occasionally someone stole from the ranchers and farmers in the region and it became necessary to take action. These incidents were usually settled peacefully, if not amicably.

In December 1858, a group of Mescaleros killed eight sheep six miles from Fort Stanton. They had an Hispano captive with them at the time. When Colonel Reeve, commanding the post, asked the captive who killed the sheep, he refused to say for fear of reprisal. Knowing the perpetrators were from Cadette's band, Reeve asked Cadette who did it. Cadette told Reeve he would inquire and inform him when he came to draw rations. When Cadette came for rations he told Reeve that he was unable to learn anything, but Reeve believed Cadette knew and intended to keep silent. Because Cadette was usually cooperative and always a strong influence for peace, Reeve concluded that to force the issue could lead to hostilities and let it drop. He decided the matter was not serious and suggested to Headquarters that the Indian agency might deal with it more effectively. Reeve also told Headquarters that if they wished to take further action, which might break the peace, he needed explicit directions from Headquarters.[87]

In January 1859, some ranchers accused Cadette's Mescaleros of stealing fifty-two mules and horses near Socorro. About the same time Indians stole several mules near El Paso, within Fort Stanton's jurisdiction. In the pursuit that followed, the thieves killed one of the pursuers. Cadette, and other White Mountain Apache leaders, claimed it was Matteo and Binanacia's band of Agua Nuevos Apaches from Dog Canyon who stole the animals. Colonel Reeve advised Headquarters that the animals could probably be recovered by demanding them, but if not, he would need directions from Headquarters. Reeve again observed that any forceful measures to recover the animals could result in hostilities. In his dispatch to Headquarters Reeve noted that it was quite possible these outrages were being committed by Comanches or Marcos' band of Mescaleros living in the Guadalupe Mountains. Marcos' band, according to Reeve, had always been hostile.[88] Reeve clearly wanted to maintain the peace.

The Mescalero Apaches had remained at peace since May 1855. Post commanders such as Captain Claiborne, Major Ruff, and Colonel Reeve tried to maintain that peace, tenuous as it was. In May 1857 Major Holmes was reluctant to send an expedition of company strength into Dog Canyon, in accordance with Department orders. A majority of the Mescalero tribe was engaged in planting crops near Dog Canyon under the direction of Indian agent Michael Steck and six men hired to teach them how to farm. Holmes wrote to Headquarters for clarification of the expedition's mission, explaining that the Indians were peaceful but were very timid. He felt that troops appearing in strength among them would alarm them and destroy their confidence in the Army's professed desire for peace. Holmes stressed that the chiefs had assured him most emphatically that they harbored no hostile Indians. When the expedition set out, Holmes directed its commander, Captain Andrew I. Lindsay, not to molest any hunting parties of Mescaleros unless clear evidence of recent depredations on their part was noted.[89]

Troops from Fort Bliss and some Mescalero Apaches did engage in a fight in Dog Canyon in February 1859. Based on information received from Major Holmes, then commanding Fort Bliss, and from Cadette, Jose Piño, Negreto, and other Apache chiefs, Major Ruff reported that the fight was with Matteo and Binanacia's bands of Mescaleros. Ruff's informants told him that the two chiefs were not involved in the fight. Unable to restrain their young men, Matteo and Binanacia had left the band. Ruff emphasized that the Mescaleros residing in the vicinity of Fort Stanton were not involved in the fight in any way. He noted that these Mescaleros offered to accompany troops in an action against those who had been engaged in the fight.[90] Cool heads prevailed and this incident did not develop into a war.

In 1861, war finally came to the homelands of the Mescaleros. However, it did not develop from any of the causes discussed here. The American Civil War pitted the white men against each other. In New Mexico, all the resources of the territory were required to fend off the Confederate assault.[91] The situation proved the theories of such men as Holmes and Ruff, who believed that it was only the presence of a strong military force at Fort Stanton that kept the Mescaleros at peace. When Union forces withdrew from Fort Stanton to face the Confederate invasion, the Mescaleros made war on the settlers in their country.[92]

Notes to Chapter I

1. Robert M. Utley, *Frontiersmen in Blue: The United States and the Indian, 1848–1865* (Lincoln: University of Nebraska Press, 1967, 1981), pp. 146–48; *Register of Letters Received and Letters Received by Headquarters, Department of New Mexico, 1854–1865,* Record Group (RG) 393, Microcopy M1120, (hereafter referred to as *Letters Received, Dept. of NM*) (Washington, DC: United States National Archives and Records Service [hereafter referred to as NARS]) roll 3, M24 through M41 for discussions between Governor Meriwether, General Garland, and others regarding the Indian problems.

2. Miles to Nichols, Jan. 5, 1855, *Letters Received, Department of NM,* roll 4, M5; James A. Bennett, *Forts and Forays, James A. Bennett: A Dragoon in New Mexico,* Clinton E. Brooks and Frank D. Reeve (eds) (Albuquerque: The University of New Mexico Press, 1948), pp. 59–60; John P. Wilson, *Merchants, Guns and Money: The Story of Lincoln County and its Wars* (Santa Fe: Museum of New Mexico Press, 1987), p. 3.

3. Bennett, pp. 60–62.

4. Wilson, *Merchants, Guns and Money,* p. 3; Miles to Nichols, Feb. 5, 1855, *Letters Received, Dept. of NM,* roll 3, M15.

5. Utley, *Frontiersmen in Blue,* pp. 146–48; Kelly R. Hays, "Fort Stanton: A History of its relations with the Mescalero Apaches" (Master's thesis, New Mexico State University, 1988), pp. 3–4; Meriwether to Garland, Jan. 29, 1855, *Letters Received, Dept. of NM,* roll 4, M11.

   Note: A company of "spies and guides" was analagous to the modern reconnaissance company. They were the trailblazers of the day.

6. Miles, to Garland, Apr. 18, 1855, *Letters Received, Dept. of NM,* roll 4, M29; Robert W. Frazer, *Forts and Supplies: The Role of the Army in the Economy of the Southwest, 1848–1861* (Albuquerque: University of New Mexico Press, 1983), p. 118; Hays, p. 6; Utley, *Frontiersmen in Blue,* p. 151.

7. Utley, *Frontiersmen in Blue,* p. 151; Hays, p. 6; Frazer, p. 118; A. B. Bender, "Frontier Defense in the Territory of New Mexico, 1853–1861," *New Mexico Historical Review,* 9 (Oct. 1934): 351; Utley, *Frontiersmen in Blue,* pp. 151–52.

8. Miles to Garland, Apr. 18, 1855, *Letters Received, Dept of NM*, roll 4, M29; Frazer, p. 118; Utley, *Frontiersmen in Blue*, pp. 151, 152.

9. Miles to Garland en route to Camp Garland, Apr. 28, 1855, *Letters Received, Dept. of NM*, roll 4, M28.

10. Ibid.

11. United States War Department, Surgeon General's Office, "Report on Barracks and Hospitals, with Descriptions of Military Posts," Circular 4, (Hereafter referred to as "Report on Barracks") (Washington, DC: United States Government Printing Office, 1870), p. 248; Extracts from two private letters written by Bvt. Major James H. Carleton and published in the *Santa Fe Gazette*, April 28, 1855, p. 2, quoted in Wilson, pp. 3–4; Miles to Garland, May 11, 1855, *Letters Received, Dept. of NM*, roll 4, M29.

12. Miles to Garland en route to Camp Garland, Apr. 28, 1855, *Letters Received, Dept. of NM*, roll 4, M28.

13. Ibid.; Francis Stanley, *Fort Stanton* (Pampa, TX: Pampa Print Shop, 1964), pp. 5, 7.

14. United States Army, *Returns from U.S. Military Posts, 1800–1916: Fort Stanton, New Mexico Only*, RG 393, Microcopy M617 (NARS), (Hereafter referred to as *Fort Stanton Returns*) roll 1216, Post Return, May, 1855; Stanley, *Fort Stanton*, p. 5.

15. Frazer, p. 118; Utley, *Frontiersmen in Blue*, pp. 151, 152; Hays, pp. 6–7; Bennett, p. 66;

16. Stanley, *Fort Stanton*, p. 5.

17. *Fort Stanton Returns*, roll 1216, Post Return, May, 1855; Frazer, pp. 118–19; "Report on Barracks" p. 248.

18. Miles to Garland, Apr. 18, 1855, and Moore to Easton, June 2, 1855, *Letters Received, Dept. of NM*, roll 4, M29, M34; Hays, p. 7; Frazer, pp. 118–19.

19. *Fort Stanton Returns*, roll 1216, Post Return, May, 1855.

20. Frazer, p. 185; Richard Greer, "Origins of the Foreign-Born Population of New Mexico During the Territorial Period," *New Mexico Historical Review*, 17 (Oct. 1942): 282.

21. W. L. Marcy, Report of the Secretary of War, 30th Congress, 1st Session, Executive Document number 23, "Report of Lt. J. W.

Albert of his Examination of New Mexico in the years 1846–47"
(Lincoln, NM: Lincoln County Heritage Trust Facsimile Reprint,
n.d.) pp. 61–62; Herb Seckler and Ken Hosmer, *Ruidoso Countryside: The Early Days* (Ruidoso: Herb Seckler and Ken Hosmer,
1987), pp. 1, 15; Wilson, *Merchants, Guns and Money*, pp. 3, 6, 7;
Warren A. Beck and Ynez D. Haas, *Historical Atlas of New Mexico*
(Norman: University of Oklahoma Press, 1969), pp. 40–42;
*Population Schedules of the Seventh Census of the United States,
1850*, Microcopy T-6, (NARS), roll 169 (hereafter referred to as
7th Census).

22. Wilson, *Merchants, Guns and Money*, pp. 1, 3–4; *Population
Schedules of the Eighth Census of the United States, 1860*,
Microcopy 653, (NARS), roll 714 (hereafter referred to as *8th
Census*).

23. Ibid.; Beck and Haas, pp. 40–42.

24. Frazer, pp. 118, 119.

25. Reeve to AAG, Dept of N.M., June 1, 1855, *Letters Received, Dept.
of NM*, roll 4, R5.

26. Reeve to AAG, Dept. of N.M., June 1, 1855, and Reeve to Easton,
July 15, 1855, *Letters Received, Dept. of NM*, roll 4, R5, R11; *Fort
Stanton Returns*, roll 1216, Post Returns, May, June, 1855; Robert
M. Utley, *Fort Union and the Santa Fe Trail* (El Paso: Texas Western
Press, 1989), pp. 8, 10–11; Utley, *Fort Union*, (Tucson: Patrice
Press), p. 50; Stanley, *Antonchico*, pp. 11, 12; *The War of the
Rebellion: A Compilation of the Official Records of the Union and
Confederate Armies*, 128 vols. (Washington, D.C.: United States
Printing Office) (hereafter referred to as *Official Records*), atlas,
part 2, plate 98, part 1, plate 54.

27. Moore to Easton, June 8, 1855, *Letters Received, Dept. of NM*, roll
4, M34.

28. Higgins to Easton, Sept. 22, 1855, and Moore to Easton, Oct. 7,
1855, *Letters Received, Dept. of NM*, roll 4, H8, M61; Frazer, p.
119.

29. Reeve to Easton, June 19, 1855, *Letters Received, Dept. of NM*, roll
4, R7.

30. Ibid.; *Fort Stanton Returns*, roll 1216, post return, June 1855.

31. Reeve to Easton, July 3, Van Horne to Easton, Aug. 4, 1855, *Letters Received, Dept. of NM,* roll 4, R10, V5.

32. Reeve to Easton, July 15 (two letters), and Van Horn to Easton, August 4, 1855, *Letters Received, Dept. of NM,* roll 4, R11, R13, V5.

33. *Fort Stanton Returns,* roll 1216, post returns, July, August, 1855; Van Horne to Easton, Aug. 4, Van Horne to Easton, Aug. 5, and Reeve to Nichols, Oct. 10, 1855, *Letters Received, Dept. of NM,* roll 4, V5, V6, R20.

34. *Fort Stanton Returns,* roll 1216, post returns, July and August, 1855; Van Horne to Easton, Aug. 13, Van Horne to Easton, Aug. 19, and Van Horne to Easton, Sept. 5, 1855, *Letters Received, Dept. of NM,* roll 4, V12, V7, and V10.

35. Ibid.; Reeve to Easton, July 3, 1855, *Letters Received, Dept. of NM,* roll 4, R10; *Fort Stanton Returns,* roll 1216, post returns, October and November, 1855.

36. Van Horne to Easton, Aug. 4, Van Horne to Easton, Aug. 5 and Reeve to Easton, July 15, 1855, *Letters Received, Dept. of NM,* roll 4, V5, V6, R13.

37. Van Horne to Nichols, Sept. 5, 1855, *Letters Received, Dept. of NM,* roll 4, V10.

38. Van Horne to Nichols, Sept. 10, 1855, *Letters Received, Dept. of NM,* roll 4, V9.

39. Van Horne to Nichols, Sept. 5, 1855, *Letters Received, Dept. of NM,* roll 4, V10.

40. Ibid.

41. Van Horne to Nichols, Sept. 21, 1855, *Letters Received, Dept. of NM,* roll 4, V13.

42. Ibid.; *Fort Stanton Returns,* roll 1216, post return, October; Van Horne to Easton, Nov. 3, 1855, *Letters Received, Dept. of NM,* Roll 4, V15.

43. Bennett, pp. 1, 75. Bennett's visit to Fort Stanton may well have been later than mid August. The editor of Bennett's diary points out that some of Bennett's dates are inaccurate. When Bennett rewrote his diary some years after he left the Army, he changed some of the dates. See p. 1.

44. Ibid.

45. Frazer, p. 118; Stanley, *Fort Stanton,* p. 200; "Report on Barracks," p. 248.

46. Ibid.; Lydia Spencer Lane, *I Married a Soldier: Or Old Days in the Old Army* (Philadelphia: Lippincott Co., 1893; repr., Albuquerque: Horn and Wallace, 1964), p. 64.

47. "Report on Barracks," p. 248–49; Lee Myers, *Fort Stanton, New Mexico: The Military Years, 1855–1896* (Lincoln, NM: Lincoln County Historical Society Publications, 1988), pp. 3–5.

48. Frazer, p. 118.

49. Bennett, p. 77.

50. "Report on Barracks," p. 248–49; Mrs Orsemus Bronson Boyd, *Cavalry Life in Tent and Field* (New York: J. S. Tait, 1894, repr. Lincoln, University of Nebraska Press, 1982) p. 169.

51. Ibid.; Van Horne to Easton, Aug. 4, 1855, and Henry to Van Horne, Aug. 4, 1855, *Letters Received, Dept. of NM,* roll 4, V5, H5.

52. Wilson, *Merchants, Guns and Money,* p. 4; Myers, pp. 3–5; Frazer, p. 172.

53. Stanley, *Fort Stanton,* p. 199.

54. Wilson, *Merchants, Guns and Money,* pp. 4, 7; Carole Gorney, "Roots in Lincoln: A History of Fort Stanton Hospital," (submitted to the New Mexico State Planning Office by the Director of New Mexico Department of Hospitals and Institutions, July, 1969, copy at Lincoln County Heritage Trust Museum), p. 8; Holmes to Nichols, April 12, 1857, *Letters Received, Dept. of NM,* roll 6, H9; *8th Census,* pp. 593–95; Frazer, p. 119.

55. Lane, p. 66; Stanley, *Fort Stanton,* pp. 7–8.

56. Ibid.

57. Reeve to Garland, June 18, 1855, *Letters Received, Dept. of NM,* roll 4, R6.

58. Ibid; *Fort Stanton Returns,* roll 1216, post return, June 1855.

59. Reeve to Easton, June 22, 1855, *Letters Received, Dept. of NM,* roll 4, R9.

60. Reeve to Easton, June 18, and Reeve to Easton June 22, 1855, *Letters Received, Dept. of NM*, roll 4, R6, R9 with enclosure.

61. Ibid.

62. Ibid.

63. Utley, *Frontiersmen in Blue*, pp. 145–48.

64. Meriwether to Garland, Jan. 29, Reeve to Easton, June 18, and Reeve to Easton, July 3, 1855, *Letters Received, Dept. of NM*, roll 4, M11, R6, R10; *Fort Stanton Returns*, roll 1216, post return, June, 1855.

65. *Fort Stanton Returns*, roll 1216, post returns, June, July, August, 1855; Van Horne, letters to Headquarters, August 19 through Sept. 13, 1855, *Letters Received, Dept. of NM*, Roll 4, V7 through V11.

Note: This order was Department of New Mexico Special Order number 71, issued August 2, 1855. It did not reach Fort Stanton until August 22.

66. Van Horne to Easton, Aug. 25, and Van Horne to Nichols, Sept. 10, 1855, *Letters Received, Dept. of NM*, roll 4, V8, V9 with inclusions; *Fort Stanton Returns*, roll 1216, post returns, August, September, 1855; Bennett, p. 75. Bear in mind that some of Bennett's dates are inaccurate. While Van Horne's, Davidson's and Bennett's accounts agree on the events, the dates given by Bennett differ from those given by Van Horne and Davidson. Bennett has the company departing Fort Stanton on August 20, Van Horne and Davidson put the date as August 28. See note 44.

67. Utley, *Frontiersmen in Blue*, pp. 151–52; Frazer, p. 118; Wilson, *Merchants, Guns and Money*, p. 4.

68. Holmes to Nichols, Apr. 12, 1857, *Letters Received, Dept. of NM*, roll 6, H9; Wilson, *Merchants, Guns and Money*, pp. 4, 7; Gorney, p. 8.

69. *Fort Stanton Returns*, roll 1216, Post Returns, March, April, 1857; Holmes to Nichols, Apr. 12, 1857, *Letters Received, Dept. of NM*, roll 6, H9; Wilson, *Merchants, Guns and Money*, pp. 4, 7; Gorney, p. 8.

70. *Fort Stanton Returns*, roll 1216, post returns, January 1859 through June 1860; Ruff to Bonneville, Feb. 2, and Ruff to AAG,

Headquarters, Dept. of NM, Feb. 21, 1859, *Letters Received, Dept. of NM*, roll 10, R8, R9.

71. *Fort Stanton Returns*, roll 1216, post returns, December 1858 through June 1861 and post returns, May 1855 through November 1857; Roberts to Canby, Aug. 2, 1861, *Official Records*, series 1, vol. 4, p. 22.

72. Frazer, pp. 114–15, 119; Moore to Easton, June 8, and Moore to Easton, Oct. 7, 1855, *Letters Received, Dept. of NM*, roll 4, M34, M61;

73. Frazer, p. 80.

74. Frazer, pp. 119, 185; Reeve to AACS, Santa Fe, Sept. 18, 1859, *Department of New Mexico Letters Sent and Received Quartermaster General Records, Commissary General Records, all New Mexico, 1848–1861* (NARS, n.d.), RG 98, 92, and 192, copy at New Mexico State Archives and Records Center, Santa Fe (hereafter referred to as *Commissary Records*).

75. Ibid.

76. Frazer, p. 119.

77. Ibid. pp. 29, 38, 72–73, 186; Wilson, *Merchants, Guns and Money*, p. 6.

78. Frazer, pp. 186–87.

79. Stanley, *Fort Stanton*, pp. 7–8.

80. Ruff to Wilkins, Sept. 16, 1859, *Letters Received, Dept. of NM*, roll 10, R38; Wilkins to Ruff, Oct. 5, 1859, *Letters Sent by the 9th Military Department, the Department of New Mexico, and the District of New Mexico, 1849–1890* RG 393, Microcopy M1072, (hereafter referred to as *Letters Sent*) (NARS), roll 2, vol. 6, #187; Wilson, *Merchants, Guns and Money*, p. 4.

81. Wilson, *Merchants, Guns and Money*, p. 4.

82. Stanley, *Fort Stanton*, p. 12.

83. Claiborne to Wilkins, Nov. 16, 1859, *Letters Received, Dept. of NM*, roll 9, C33.

84. Robert M. Utley, *Frontier Regulars: The United States Army and the Indian, 1866–1891* (New York: Macmillan Publishing Co. Inc., 1973), p. 90; Don R. Rickey, Jr., *Forty Miles a Day on Beans and*

Hay: The Enlisted Soldier Fighting the Indian Wars (Norman: University of Oklahoma Press, 1963), pp. 168–69; Monroe Lee Billington, *New Mexico's Buffalo Soldiers, 1866–1900* (Niwot, CO: University Press of Colorado, 1991) pp. 36, 115.

85. Claiborne to Wilkins, Nov. 16, 1859, *Letters Received, Dept. of NM,* roll 9, C33.

86. Ruff to Wilkins, Sept. 23, 1859, *Letters Received, Dept. of NM,* roll 10, R38.

87. Reeve to Wilkins, Jan. 5, 1859, *Letters Received, Dept. of NM,* roll 10, R3.

88. Reeve to Wilkins, Jan 12, 1859, *Letters Received, Dept. of NM,* roll 10, R4.

89. Wilson, *Merchants, Guns and Money,* pp. 4, 6, 9; Holmes to Nichols, May 12, and Holmes to Nichols, July 5, 1857, *Letters Received, Dept. of NM,* roll 6, H14, H20 enclosure 1.

90. Ruff to AAG, Feb. 21, 1859, *Letters Received, Dept. of NM,* roll 10, R9.

91. Utley, *Frontiersmen in Blue,* p. 174.

92. Holmes to Nichols, Apr. 12, 1857, and Ruff to Bonneville, Feb. 2, 1859, *Letters Received, Dept. of NM,* roll 6, H9, roll 10, R8; Utley, *Frontiersmen in Blue,* p. 174.

Chapter II

THE CIVIL WAR YEARS

In April 1861, Confederate forces opened fire on Fort Sumter and the Civil War began. The Civil War caused the cessation of military efforts to subdue the Indians in the Southwest, and the influx of settlers to the region slackened as well. The entire military resources of New Mexico were required to deal with the Confederate invasion. The Indians of the Territory, noting the preoccupation of the whites with their civil war, took advantage of the situation to try to rid their lands of the white settlers.[1]

As early as February 1861, Captain Carter S. Stevenson, commanding Fort Stanton, reported that the Mescaleros had joined forces with the Mimbres Apaches and were prosecuting a war against the settlers. Troops from Fort Stanton took some action against the hostile Mescaleros late in March, but in May several officers resigned their commissions and departed Fort Stanton, leaving only Captain, Bvt. Ltc., Benjamin S. Roberts and Lt. Edward Cressy. Colonel Roberts assumed command of the post. In June, Roberts assumed command of the Independent Regiment of Mounted Rifles under similar circumstances.

On June 24, Roberts reported that hostilities with the Mescaleros were a certainty. He stated that Manco, Manuelito and Cadette were determined to keep to their agreement, but that they could no longer control either the other leaders or their own young men. Roberts explained that his force was too small to deal with an Indian uprising and he could not protect the settlements in such an event. He requested more troops, regardless of the threat of invasion from Texas, to help deal with the Mescaleros.[2]

Events throughout the Department were similar until the Civil War itself came to New Mexico. Starting in March and continuing through June 1861, a number of ranking officers in the Department of New Mexico resigned their commissions in the United States Army to serve the Confederacy. On June 18 raiders overpowered the post herders at Fort Fillmore, stealing thirty-nine of the cavalry horses. Authorities at the post suspected Confederate sympathizers of the crime. The thieves took the horses to Texas where they were again stolen, this time by Mexican bandits who took them to Mexico. Meanwhile, Ltc. Isaac Lynde, commanding Fort Fillmore, obtained fifty replacements from Fort Craig. Ltc. Edward R. S. Canby took command of the department on June 22, 1861. On July 25 Ltc. John R. Baylor, Confederate States Army, with 258 men, invaded New Mexico Territory and captured the town of Mesilla. Baylor had planned a surprise attack on Fort Fillmore, but a deserter from his command warned the garrison. Baylor altered his plans and occupied the town of Mesilla instead. The citizens of Mesilla, unhappy with the Federal Government, were only too happy to embrace the Confederate cause. Colonel Lynde made a feeble attempt to retake the town, but Baylor's forces had the full cooperation and assistance of the citizens of Mesilla. When Lynde's attempt to retake Mesilla failed, he withdrew to Fort Fillmore and prepared to abandon the post.[3] On July 27, Lynde quit Fort Fillmore, retreating toward Fort Stanton. Baylor received word of Lynde's retreat and overtook him at San Augustine Pass that same day. Lynde's troops, against orders, had filled their canteens with whiskey and suffered miserably during the retreat from thirst and exhaustion in the intense heat. Able to field only a hundred men capable of fighting, Lynde surrendered.[4] At the time of surrender Lynde's command included troops from Fort Stanton on detached service. Forty men of Lynde's command managed to avoid capture.[5]

On August 2, one of the soldiers who evaded capture at San Augustine Pass arrived at Fort Stanton and told Lieutenant Colonel Roberts of Lynde's surrender. Colonel Canby had ordered the commanders of Forts Craig and Stanton to withdraw as soon as the troops retreating from the south passed by. Roberts understood that five hundred Confederate troops were advancing on Fort Stanton, when in fact

Baylor had only about half that number in his entire command. In compliance with orders, and believing his force to be substantially outnumbered, Roberts immediately took action to abandon Fort Stanton. He sent the man who brought him word of the surrender at San Augustine Pass to Headquarters in Santa Fe with the news of Lynde's surrender and of his own abandonment of Fort Stanton. Roberts then ordered all public stores that could not be taken destroyed and the post set afire. Finally, he dispatched two companies of infantry to Albuquerque and proceeded to Santa Fe with two companies of cavalry.[6]

That night a rainstorm put out the fires. Baylor reported that a group of "...citizens living near the fort..." occupied the fort and saved much of the supplies and commissary stores. The *Mesilla Times* reported that these "citizens" were a group of about forty Arizonans who took possession of the fort in the name of the Confederacy and immediately sent an express to Mesilla to ask for help in protecting the stores and property. According to Baylor, "Indians and Mexicans," probably residents of the region, gathered in a large force and demanded the right to pillage the fort. The "citizens," too weak to defend the post, and not knowing if they could expect help from the Confederate troops in Mesilla, abandoned the post.[7]

On August 10, Colonel Baylor received word of the abandonment of Fort Stanton and dispatched Capt. James Walker with his company to occupy the post. Though the fort had been pillaged, Walker managed to recover most of the provisions and four field pieces. Baylor sent a wagon train to take what stores and supplies he could from the fort, leaving only two months' provisions for Walker's troops. This train left for Fort Bliss on August 30. Two of the four cannon at Fort Stanton were serviceable and Baylor reported that all the captured arms he had could be put into working condition.[8] Gen. Henry H. Sibley had plans for Fort Stanton. He wanted the fort as a relay station to the Mesilla Valley, and as a supply depot for troops moving into and out of the Confederate Territory of Arizona, established by Colonel Baylor on August 1, 1861. Baylor's reason for sending troops to the post was more mundane; he feared for the safety of the families in the area.[9]

Baylor's feeling that the people near Fort Stanton needed protection was well founded. The Indians of New Mexico, now unrestrained by the U. S. Army, were vigorously prosecuting their war on white settlers. Virtually every issue of the *Mesilla Times* for 1861 features articles about Indian depredations. On July 15, Apaches killed Richmond Jones, Edward Tarbox, a man named McCall, two Hispanics, and an Indian boy near Mesilla. On August 10, the *Mesilla Times* complained bitterly that the Apaches were committing murders and depredations almost daily throughout the territory with impunity. In one instance, the California mail run was attacked by Apaches near Cook Springs. The mail was taken, and seven men were killed. The August 17 issue of the *Mesilla Times* reported that the San Antonio and San Diego (SA & SD) mail route was discontinued due to Indian activity in the region. An article in the *Mesilla Times* proposed arming the Pima and Papago Indians. Supposedly these "civilized" tribes would gladly fight the hated Apaches for the plunder they could get.[10]

In September, twenty-five men returned to the Rio Bonito area to harvest the crops they had abandoned when Confederate troops invaded from Texas. The men were never heard from again. It is highly likely that these men are the men referred to in a Texas newspaper article detailing how a group of men, who had returned to the Rio Bonito to harvest their crops, was massacred near Fort Stanton. The year 1862 was no better. According to Indian Agent Don Lorenzo Labadi, during the month of August alone, the Apaches killed forty men and six children in South-Central New Mexico, taking others into captivity. Labadi reported that, unless the government took immediate steps, the countryside would be completely stripped of everything of value.[11]

The presence of Confederate troops at Fort Stanton did not act as a deterrent to Indian outrages, and the Indians were more than Baylor's small force could cope with. Shortly after occupying the fort, Captain Walker went to Fort Bliss, leaving Lt. John R. Pulliam in command of the post. Pulliam sent a four-man detail to the Gallinas Mountains to get water. Because of Indian activity in the region, Pulliam ordered the men not to remain near the water hole and to "...noon at a safe and sufficient distance away..." This order was disobeyed, and the men camped in a conspicuous location above the spring where their campfire was clearly visible. They were attacked by a band of Apaches and a two-hour running fight ensued in which three of the men were killed.[12]

Colonel Baylor complained to his superiors that he did not have enough men to deal with the Indians and defend the territory against

Union forces, but received no reenforcements. He had invaded New Mexico with only 258 men. A few had deserted and some had been killed or wounded, including the water detail at Fort Stanton and fourteen men lost attacking a Mescalero camp. Baylor expected an attack by a column of 240 Union troops from Fort Craig imminently and, although the attack never materialized, he was compelled to make preparations. Needing every man he could get, Baylor decided to abandon Fort Stanton. Baylor, who had spent most of September at Fort Bliss, gave verbal instructions to Captain Walker to abandon Fort Stanton upon his return. When Walker returned to Fort Stanton, late in the evening of September 1, he had his troops begin preparations to evacuate the fort. On the evening of September 8, just before the Confederates were to depart, word came that Indians were attacking La Placita. Walker sent Lieutenant Pulliam with fifteen men to help defend the town. Pulliam drove the Indians off after a hard fight in which five Indians were killed. He returned to Fort Stanton at 2:00 AM, September 9, in a heavy rainstorm. The next morning Walker's command, having occupied Fort Stanton for less than a month, abandoned the post and returned to Mesilla. By September 10, 1861, Fort Stanton was again vacant. Late in September, Colonel Canby sent a company of spies and guides to the vicinity of Fort Stanton to determine the exact state of affairs in the region, but no one made an attempt to reoccupy the fort. Most of the settlers in the area fled as quickly as possible.[13]

On March 28, 1862, the Union and Confederate forces in New Mexico engaged in a significant battle in Glorieta Pass. During the battle a small force of Union troops, trying to get behind Confederate lines, found and attacked the Confederate supply train, destroying it completely. When the Confederate commander, who was winning the fight, received word of the loss of his train, he offered a truce. The Union commander accepted and withdrew his battered forces. Even though the Confederate forces prevailed at Glorieta, they were compelled to withdraw for lack of supplies. On April 15, at Peralta, Confederate forces engaged Union forces in a rear guard action. After Confederate forces withdrew in 1862, they made no further attempts to take New Mexico.[14] In the meantime, Gen. James H. Carleton, commanding a column of California Volunteers, marched across the Arizona desert to help combat the Confederate invasion.[15]

41

Brevet Brigadier General James H. Carleton
Courtesy Museum of New Mexico, Neg. No. 22938

Carleton arrived in Santa Fe on September 16, 1862, after Confederate forces had retreated from New Mexico Territory. Carleton assumed command of the Department of New Mexico on September 18, relieving Col. Edward R. S. Canby, who was transferred to the fighting in the East. The Navajos and Apaches raided unchecked throughout the Territory of New Mexico, and the Kiowas and Comanches raided the eastern fringes of the territory and attacked parties on the Santa Fe Trail. Carleton planned an all-out war on the Indians, especially the Navajos and Apaches. He believed it would be best to station troops in the heart of Mescalero and Navajo country and operate from there. To provide troops for his Indian campaigns Carleton dismantled the small posts of Gallisteo, Los Lunas, Polvadero, and Cubero. The troops from these posts garrisoned Forts Wingate, in Navajo country, and Stanton, in Mescalero country.[16]

Carleton decided to operate first against those he believed to be the worst offenders, the Mescalero Apaches. On September 27 General Carleton ordered Col. Christopher (Kit) Carson, commanding the 1st New Mexico Volunteer Regiment, to take five companies of infantry from his regiment to Fort Stanton and reopen that post. Four of the companies were to be mounted. Carson was to proceed directly to the fort, diverting only to Fort Union for supplies. Carson's assignment was to subdue the Mescalero Apaches and keep watch for a possible invasion along the Pecos River from Fort Lancaster, Texas.[17]

The first troops of Carson's command arrived at Fort Stanton on October 17, 1862. They were the two companies commanded by Capt. James Graydon and Capt. John Thompson. Maj. Arthur Morrison arrived on October 23 with Capt. Edward H. Bergmen and his company. Colonel Carson and 1st Lt. Joseph S. Berney arrived at Fort Stanton on October 26. These were the first Union troops to occupy the post since Colonel Roberts had abandoned it in August 1861. The fort had been vacant for fourteen months, and Carson reported finding it a shambles. In some places only bare walls were standing. The once commodious and sturdy Fort Stanton was now one of the most dilapidated posts in New Mexico and offered little hope of shelter before winter. At least four companies of New Mexico Volunteers were to call this place home for some time to come, and Lieutenant Berney had to get the fort into habitable condition. He managed to get one room roofed and rigged as a commissary and quartermaster's storeroom, but the troops had to make do with Sibley tents. The command had no vegetables or flour. As of October 31, the beef herd had not arrived, and feed for the

Civilian Christopher Carson
Courtesy Kit Carson Memorial Foundation, Inc.

horses was in short supply.[18]

On October 30, Carson complained that he had only 20,000 pounds of corn, which would last him about fifteen days. In a letter written October 17, he stated that he had only been able to get 30,000 pounds at Fort Union, which would only last fifteen to twenty days at half rations. The grass in the vicinity of Fort Stanton was insufficient for the horses because of a recent drought. Carson said that if his horses had to subsist on the available ration for long they would be useless. He asked General Carleton to direct the Quartermaster Department to forward corn to him in time for his campaign or to authorize Lieutenant Berney to purchase it locally. Carson believed he could obtain a sufficient supply of corn through local entrepreneurs, including Dr. John M. Whitlock and Mr. John Dold. Carson knew Whitlock and Dold personally and they had assured Carson that they could provide the needed corn.[19]

Most of the farms and settlements near Fort Stanton had been abandoned at the outbreak of the Civil War. Although most of the settlers who fled never returned, some hardy souls did come back in time to harvest crops. Lieutenant Berney, in need of commissary and subsistence stores, was able to purchase some items locally. This was beneficial to both parties. The post had money, or memorandums of receipt, and needed supplies and the citizens needed a market for their goods. However, until Colonel Carson could eliminate the Indian menace, the prospects of a growing population in the area would remain poor.[20]

Carson had his hands full. General Carleton had ordered him to station troops at the junction of the Hondo and Pecos Rivers to watch for signs of a possible invasion from Fort Lancaster in Texas, along the Pecos River.

Colonel Christopher Carson
Courtesy Kit Carson Historic Museum

Carson had to establish a permanent camp and place an entire company there. Because the camp was a considerable distance from Fort Stanton, these troops could not help with any of the other activities of the garrison. Carson's orders also required him to chastise the Indians, who surrounded him. Carson knew that chastising the Indians would keep the bulk of his remaining four companies constantly in the field. Thus, Carson's troops had little time to spend repairing the fort. Winters in the Sacramento Mountains are harsh and Carson requested that another company be sent to Fort Stanton so some repairs could be made. General Carleton expected Carson to chastise the Mescaleros with just three of his companies, leaving the fourth at the fort. Carleton did not provide the additional company.[21]

The rules laid down by Carleton for his war on the hostile Indians were harsh. En route to Fort Stanton Carson received a confidential communication from Carleton instructing him to kill all Indian men whenever and wherever they were encountered. The women and children were not to be harmed, but rather taken prisoner and fed at Fort Stanton until Carson received instructions regarding their disposition. If the Mescaleros sought peace they were to be told that because of their treachery in breaking the peace when the white man was engaged in a war, they were no longer to be trusted. Carson was there to kill them and had no power to make peace. He was to tell the Mescaleros that if they wanted peace, their chiefs and twenty of their principle men must go to Santa Fe to talk with General Carleton, and that Carson would keep killing them until he received orders from Santa Fe to stop.[22]

These harsh rules applied to all the tribes engaged in hostile activities in the territory. Carleton's instructions for the commander of Fort Bascom were to send away all white flags of the Kiowas and Comanches unless they were willing to give up all stolen property. Even then they had to go to Santa Fe Headquarters to surrender and were prohibited from visiting either the Navajos or the Apaches in the interim. Furthermore, hostilities would continue to be prosecuted until their surrender had been accepted at Santa Fe. Regarding the Navajos, Carleton believed that talks would have no effect and they would have to be defeated and taught to fear the Army, before they would stop their depredations. As with the Mescaleros, Navajo men were to be killed whenever and wherever encountered, and women and children were to be taken prisoner. The killing would continue until the Navajo leaders made peace with Carleton in Santa Fe.[23]

Carleton put a high priority on the subjugation of the Apaches and applied substantial resources to the task. When Carleton took charge of the Department of New Mexico, Col. Joseph R. West assumed command of the District of Arizona, which included southern New Mexico. However, Carleton remained Military Governor of Arizona, giving him executive powers over the District. Using those powers, Carleton directed Colonel West to send two expeditions against the Mescalero Apaches. The commanders of these two expeditions were to be Captains William McCleave and Thomas L. Roberts. Carson's command at

Fort Stanton, in the heart of Mescalero country, was to be the trap into which McCleave and Roberts would drive the prey. Believing that the best time to operate against the Indians was in the winter, Carleton directed that the expeditions were to commence on November 15, 1862, and remain in the field until December 31. Each expedition was to be composed of two companies, twenty scouts and spies, and one surgeon. Because of concern that the Confederates might launch another invasion of New Mexico, Carleton sent copies of the orders to each of the three commanders, with maps of the area to be covered, so that each would be aware of the presence and movements of the others and not mistake them for Confederates.[24]

To insure that these expeditions had everything they needed, Carleton sent his best Quartermaster and Commissary officer, Capt. Nicholas S. Davis, to work for Colonel West. Carleton advised West that he was sending funds with Captain Davis taken from the California Volunteers' accounts. If West needed money for anything before the funds arrived he was to borrow it from the Subsistence Department. Carson was provided with funds from the New Mexico Volunteers accounts and an especially large force of men, to use as he saw fit, provided they vigorously prosecuted the war against the Mescaleros. To ensure that his plans were not frustrated from the start, Carleton cautioned all parties to secrecy until after they had departed on their missions so that the Indians would not get word and vanish. In fact, Carleton had received peace feelers from Mangus Coloradas in September but did not trust him. Carleton wrote to Colonel West advising him of that fact and pointed out that he wanted to punish Mangus Coloradas, who had been particularly vicious around the Pinos Altos Mines. Carleton directed West to personally lead a scout in the Pinos Altos region for the specific purpose of punishing Mangus Coloradas.[25]

All the preparation and secrecy may not have been necessary in the case of the Mescaleros. Before Carson even reached Fort Stanton, one incident, which had wide-ranging repercussions, nearly brought the war against the Mescaleros to an end before it began. On October 18, 1862, Captain James Graydon, 1st Mounted New Mexico Volunteers, attacked the camp of Mescalero chief Manuelito and killed eleven Indians, including the chiefs Manuelito and José Largo. The attacking troops wounded twenty Mescaleros and took two children captive. Graydon appropriated the Indians' horses for his own command and destroyed the camp. Although this incident hastened the capitulation of the Mescaleros, it did not win Graydon any friends. Carson had met with Manuelito in September and believed the chief sincere in his desire for peace. Major Morrison made a detailed report regarding Manuelito's death in which he accused Graydon of treachery and improper conduct. Carson ordered an investigation, but before the investigation could be completed Graydon and Dr. John M. Whitlock were dead.

Whitlock was a La Placita physician and entrepreneur. He and John Dold promised Carson that they could provide corn for the post and Carson was trying to get permission to contract with them for the coming year. In addition, Whitlock had served in Carson's regiment as a surgeon until the regiment was reorganized in May 1862. He personally knew Carson and Manuelito. The *Santa Fe Weekly Gazette* published a letter from Whitlock accusing Graydon of treachery and murder in the death of Manuelito, and Graydon resented the accusations.[26] Whitlock came to Fort Stanton in early November to talk to Carson regarding a position as surgeon in Carson's command. While at the fort, Whitlock encountered Graydon and an argument ensued concerning the published letter. The two men shot each other. Seeing their commander wounded, Graydon's company rioted, killing Whitlock. Graydon died of his wounds four days later, on November 9.[27]

The death of Manuelito upset many, both white and Indian, because he was known to be a peace advocate and was purported to be on his way to Santa Fe to make peace when he was killed. Manuelito had been talking peace for some time, but he had not taken positive action beyond talking. Carleton reminded his subordinates that no council would be held with the Indians and they must rigidly follow this order. Manuelito's death, coupled with the activities of Captains McCleave and Roberts in the field, served notice that Carleton's war was not going to be put off by talk.[28]

On October 27, Cadette came to Fort Stanton seeking peace and Carson directed him to Santa Fe. Dissatisfied with Carleton's terms for peace as explained by Carson, Cadette did not go to Santa Fe. In November, driven by Captain McCleave's operations in Dog Canyon and Carson's operations in the Sacramento Mountains, Cadette again came to Fort Stanton seeking peace. This time Cadette, Chato and Estrella escorted by Indian Agent Lorenzo Labadi, went to Santa Fe, leaving a hundred Mescaleros camped at the fort awaiting the outcome of the negotiations. In Santa Fe the chiefs maintained they had always been opposed to those Mescaleros who were committing depredations and wished to live in peace. Carleton told the three chiefs that if they truly wished to live in peace they would have to move their people to Fort Union or a reservation at Bosque Redondo and have no communications with the other bands. The chiefs reluctantly agreed to move their people to Bosque Redondo. Carleton had established the Bosque Redondo reservation earlier that year as an experiment in teaching the Mescaleros and Navajos how to farm. Near the reservation, on the east bank of the Pecos River, Fort Sumner watched over the reservation and acted as a defense against Kiowa and Comanche Indians raiding into eastern New Mexico.[29]

Cadette may not have been as completely reformed as he would have Carleton believe. By December 14 Carson had more than 240 Indians, including sixty Navajos, camped near the fort. When Carson told them he would have to move them to Mora instead of Bosque Redondo if the Confederate forces invaded again, Cadette asked Carson's permission to raid the Confederates and steal their stock. Carson thought it was a good idea and recommended it to Carleton.[30]

On December 24, all Indians camped near the fort left for Bosque Redondo with a wagon train and escorted by agent Labadi. By mid-January 1863 another large group of Indians was camped near Fort Stanton and Carleton ordered Carson to send them to Bosque Redondo without delay and report in person to Santa Fe.[31] In a January 4 report Carson, confident that reasons no longer existed for people to stay away from the region, stated that Indians then coming to the fort constituted the last of the Mescalero Apaches not already at Bosque Redondo. Carson boasted that since the arrival of his command at Fort Stanton, several ranches and grazing camps had been established in the area and none had experienced any incidents with Indians.[32]

Carleton, who had been at Fort Stanton when it was first built, knew the area was fertile and wanted to see it settled by industrious farmers, ranchers, and miners. Prior to Carson's January report Carleton had inaugurated an extensive public relations campaign to get people to return to the Bonito, Ruidoso, and Tularosa river valleys. Carleton provided newspapers with some of Carson's letters regarding the conditions in the area. In one letter, published in the *Santa Fe Weekly Gazette*, Carson announced the region had been subdued and it "...begins to assume the appearance of industry and civilization." Carson stated that 150 miners were now working at the gold mines in the vicinity of Fort Stanton. In this letter Carson encouraged people to settle along the Bonito, Ruidoso, and Tularosa Rivers.[33]

The settlers, on the other hand, wanted assurance that the Army would protect them. The Colorado Volunteers, who had driven Confederate forces from New Mexico, were still in the territory but rumors of their withdrawal were causing concern throughout New Mexico. If the number of troops in the territory were reduced then the size of the garrisons at posts such as Fort Stanton would have to be reduced, limiting their effectiveness against hostile Indians. The editor of the *Santa Fe Gazette* complained that General Carleton was doing his best but needed an additional regiment instead of losing one. The editorial emphasized that partial punishment of the Indians was worse than no punishment at all and the transfer of troops would leave settlers open to further depredations.[34]

By February 1, 1863, all Colorado Volunteers had been ordered home, and Carleton complained he did not have enough troops to fight more than one tribe at a time. By this date, over 350 Mescaleros resided at Fort Sumner, or were on their way there. Once the Mescaleros at Bosque Redondo learned to farm and raise stock, Carleton planned to move them to a reservation near Fort Stanton. Believing all but a small number of Mescaleros were accounted for, Carleton was assembling troops in preparation for his Navajo campaign.[35] On February 3, Colonel Carson submitted his resignation. Carleton did not accept the resignation but allowed Carson to go home for an extended leave.[36]

On March 19, Maj. Arthur Morrison, commanding Fort Stanton since Carson's departure, left to assume command at Mesilla, taking one company with him. The Fort Stanton garrison, including the troops on picket duty at the junction of the Hondo and Pecos rivers, now consisted of four under-strength companies with Capt. Francisco P. Abreu commanding the fort and two of the companies. Since Carleton had begun shifting troops for service in the Navajo campaign, the aggregate number of troops at Fort Stanton had fallen from 301 to 143. By May only two companies occupied the fort.[37]

Also on March 19, Carleton reported to the Adjutant General of the Army that approximately four hundred Mescalero men, women, and children were at Bosque Redondo. Although about a hundred Mescaleros had fled to Mexico or united with the Gila Apaches, Carleton believed the Mescaleros had been subdued. Because farms and ranches now dotted the region, he changed his mind about placing the Mescaleros on a reservation near Fort Stanton. Carleton told the Adjutant General that Indians should be placed on reservations far removed from white settlements so whites could possess the good agricultural and mineral bearing land and exploit it without interference from Indians. Carleton believed if the Mescaleros returned to their homelands, they would take up raiding once more and would have to be subdued again, at great cost. Only force and intimidation would keep the Mescaleros from raiding, and he intended to keep them where they could be watched and forced to farm. Carleton planned to have the Mescaleros plant a crop that spring and to have the Catholic Bishop of Santa Fe, John Baptist Lamy, send a priest to teach the tribe Christianity and open a school for the children. He intended to turn the Mescaleros into what he called a *pueblo*, a compliant, sedentary, colony of farmers. To obtain the services of a resident priest, Carleton had to have Fort Sumner declared a Chaplain Post. He obtained the classification and Bishop Lamy sent a priest to Fort Sumner.[38]

The campaign against the Mescaleros was short but effective, resulting in the concentration of more than four hundred members of the tribe on the Bosque Redondo reservation at Fort Sumner before the end of March 1863.[39] Within a year of Fort Stanton's reopening more than 100 families had moved into the region and were farming and prospecting there.[40]

The growth of settlement in the region was not as rapid as Carleton might have wished, however, due to continued Indian activity in the area. Even though Carleton declared that the war with the Mescaleros was over on March 19, 1863, Mescalero holdouts continued to raid and plunder. Navajos, uninhibited by a strong Mescalero population, also began to roam and raid in the former Mescalero lands. In addition, the Mescaleros at Bosque Redondo remained only a relatively short time before they began to leave in small groups, returning to the mountains in southeast New Mexico and Northern Mexico.[41] As a result, the garrison at Fort Stanton was kept busy throughout 1863 and 1864 trying to protect local settlers and round up the Indians.[42]

As if to symbolize their defiance in the face of Carleton's March 19 pronouncement, a band of Mescaleros attacked a salt train near Fort Stanton on March 24, stealing seventy head of cattle. Two men, wounded and left for dead, survived. Carleton issued orders that any Mescalero men attempting to leave Bosque Redondo were to be shot. If another incident like the salt train occurred, the entire tribe was to be moved to Fort Union after being disarmed, including bows and arrows, and all their animals confiscated. Carleton also ordered the "Commanding Officer, Fort Stanton," to kill any Mescalero men found in the vicinity without a written pass from the commander of Fort Sumner. Any women and children encountered were to be taken to Fort Sumner as prisoners and warned that if they returned without a written pass they would be shot. Carleton stipulated that Capt. Francisco P. Abreu was to recover the remains of the salt train and return them to their owner. Abreu, commanding the post, took a detail to recover the remains of the train, leaving Lt. William Brady temporarily in command of the post.[43] Finally, Carleton instructed the post commander to keep detachments in the Sacramento and Sierra Blanca Mountains at all times in search of Indians, promising additional troops for that purpose when reinforcements arrived.[44] Meanwhile, the undermanned garrison at Fort Stanton remained hard pressed.

By late March, Navajos were regularly making attacks on the lines of communication between Fort Union and Fort Stanton. Abreu sent escorts with all express riders bound for Santa Fe through the Gallinas Mountains because of the danger. Late in March, a band of about forty Navajos, with a large herd of sheep, unsuccessfully attacked two express riders leaving Fort Stanton for Fort Union. This was probably the same band that had stolen six thousand sheep in Texas less than a month before and eluded pursuit. Abreu immediately sent Lt. David McAllister with thirty men to the Sierra Oscuras to intercept these Indians and recover the sheep. The raiders evaded McAllister and dispersed in the mountainous terrain.[45]

Where the Army was not successful, the people of the settlements sometimes were. On May 1, Captain Abreu took fifteen men to search for Indians who had been raiding along the Rio Tularosa. He traveled across the Ruidoso River, along the Carrizo River and over to Tularosa, returning to Fort Stanton by way of Ojo de las Sernilas and McGowan's Ranch. Abreu covered 260 miles, returning to Fort Stanton on May 10, but saw no Indians. However, a party of forty Hispanos, lead by one E. Duran, followed the trail of the Indians into the mountains near Fort Stanton from the settlement of Tularosa. Duran's force surprised the Indians, killed fourteen and wounded an undetermined number. Duran's party captured ten wagon-loads of dried meat and some of the property taken during the salt train attack on March 24. The Hispanos suffered two men killed and one wounded. Major Joseph Smith, who had taken command at Fort Stanton on the first of May, told Duran to bring his wounded man to the hospital at Fort Stanton for treatment.[46]

A pattern was emerging, whereby the Indians would follow a circuitous route attacking a number of scattered points within a short period of time. They then retreated to remote mountain reaches where it was difficult to follow. On May 16, Indians raided the farms along the Ruidoso River. At one farm, nine miles from Fort Stanton, they stole ten or twelve head of stock, killing one man and ransacking his house. Upon receiving word of the raid Smith sent 2nd Lt. William H. Higden with ten men to the scene. Higden ascertained that about thirty Indians had raided the farm but was unable to catch them. After burying the farmer, Higden returned to the post and Smith sent 2nd Lt. Thomas Henderson with twelve men to find the trail and follow it. The raiders' trail led into the mountains south of Ruidoso and, circuitously, to La Placita, where they raided again. The citizens of La Placita sent word of the raid to Smith, who sent Lieutenant Higden and ten men to their aid. When they left La Placita, the raiders went into the Sierra Capitans, where neither Henderson nor Higden were able to follow.[47]

In a letter to headquarters Smith pointed out that he had only two companies and was required to keep one company on picket duty and to assign men to watch over a large post herd. These requirements, coupled with poor horses, meant that Smith could not send enough men after raiding Indians to have any real hope of success. Smith stated that his entire garrison had been on scouts for the last four days and requested another company. This would enable him to pursue hostile Indians more effectively.[48]

In June, the Indians began raiding frequently at widely scattered locations. The troops at Fort Stanton were unable to gain control of the situation. On June 20, a band of Mescaleros attacked Capt. Albert H. Pfeiffer's company of New Mexico Volunteers near Fort McRae. On June 21, a band of Navajos attacked the express to Fort Stanton from Santa Fe, taking their mules and all the mail. When Navajos raided the post herd on June 26, taking sixty horses and mules, Smith immediately took a detail in pursuit. The next day, he encountered Captain Abreu pursuing the same band, which had raided the mail on the twenty-first. At this point the entire garrison was in the field and Smith returned to the post with the infantry.[49] Late in June Indians captured the express riders bringing the mail from Fort Stanton to Santa Fe and tortured them to death by fire. This incident incensed Carleton, who ordered any Indian men at large in the area without a pass killed and emphasized that the troops were to show no mercy. He transferred Capt. Emil Fritz's company of cavalry to Fort Stanton and instructed Smith to use Fritz's troops in details, with one officer in command of each detail.[50]

On July 2, Carleton directed that Captain Abreu's company, scheduled to transfer from Fort Stanton, march at once. Smith complained that without Abreu's company he did not have enough men to pursue and chastise the Indians. His horses were poor, he needed another company of infantry—even with Abreu's company, he could not mount more than twenty men at a time.[51] Throughout July conditions remained unchanged. The post herd was raided more than once and the picket post on the Pecos was surrounded and attacked. Carleton decided to place a large garrison at Fort Stanton. On July 29, he instructed Smith to keep Abreu's company at the fort, recall the pickets at the Pecos River, and direct all his attention to hunting and killing Indians. In addition, Carleton sent Company C, 7th Infantry, with instructions that it was to be kept in the field until the Indian problems were eliminated. Carleton admonished Smith to take the initiative and devise a way to surprise the Indians and destroy them.[52] The raids continued through August, even though Smith kept scouts in the field constantly. Company C arrived on August 26 and Smith wrote to Headquarters the same day promising to keep the troops in the field.[53]

Smith's command at the end of August included New Mexico Volunteers, California Volunteers and regulars. Carleton advised Smith to encourage competition between them, reasoning that it would result in a more thorough scouring of the Sierra Blanca, Capitan, and Sacramento Mountains. This worked for a time, but, in May 1864, serious trouble developed between the regulars and the New Mexico Volunteers. The regulars considered themselves professionals and, therefore, superior to volunteers. Because of this they expected preferential treatment and ignored the Hispano officers of the New Mexico Volunteers, often to the point of insubordination. Racial attitudes obviously motivated much of the troubles because the regulars and California Volunteers, who were Anglo, did not have this problem.[54] Clearly, the situation contributed to the difficulties the garrison experienced in catching and punishing hostile Indians.

September showed a marked improvement in the situation. Smith, true to his word, kept two or more scouts in the field at a time and personally led several scouts. These scouts found evidence of Indians, and even some Indian dead, but nothing encountered was more recent than six weeks. Early in September Carleton asked Smith if he still needed Company C. Smith responded that his last two scouts had found no signs of Indians, but he did not know how long that would last. Smith wanted to keep Company C because Captain Fritz and his company, some junior officers, and a detachment of enlisted men were departing the post and he did not want to be reduced to a two-company post again. Carleton ordered Company C sent to the Gallinas Mountains to clean out and improve Gallinas Spring, roughly ninety miles from Fort Stanton on the road to Fort Union via Anton Chico. They were to remain in the field until December 1, attacking any Indians they encountered. On September 19, Capt. George S. Hollister, commanding Company C, departed with his command for Gallinas Spring.[55]

In addition to Company C, the expedition included fifteen cavalrymen of Company A, 1st Cavalry, New Mexico Volunteers. On the evening of September 22 one of Hollister's pickets saw six Indians at Gallinas Spring. The next day, Hollister left Company C camped at the spring and took the cavalry unit in pursuit of the Indians seen by the picket. They did not catch the Indians, but Hollister noted that their trail led toward Fort Sumner.[56]

On September 25, Smith left Fort Stanton to join the expedition at Gallinas Spring. Except for the Indians pursued on the twenty-third, no indications of any Indian presence could be found. The troops built a tank at Gallinas Spring sufficient for five hundred horses and then moved to Patos Spring, about a day's march from Fort Stanton on the Anton Chico Road, and improved that spring as well. At Patos Spring the tank was large enough for five hundred horses, but Smith reported that the water supply would be insufficient for some time. Nor was any water to be found between Gallinas Spring and Patos Spring, a distance of sixty miles. On October 1, as a backup supply for large commands, Smith ordered Hollister to build a tank sufficient for five hundred horses four miles below Patos Spring. Company C departed Fort Stanton on November 20, having completed the tank below Patos Spring.[57]

While at Gallinas Spring Smith, pursuant to orders from Carleton, looked for gold while the troops worked on the spring. He did not find gold but reported that the region had potential, citing specific locations as promising. Carleton used reports of good prospects, such as Smith's, to encourage prospecting in the area, bringing miners to the region.[58]

Besides attracting miners and other settlers, the work of the troops at Fort Stanton yielded other important benefits to the community. Improving the springs and building tanks for military purposes also benefited commercial enterprise and the many citizens who used the springs. Like the military, freighters needed water for their animals. In addition to public works such as roads, springs, and tanks, the Army provided much needed economic support. The garrison at Fort Stanton purchased goods and services, providing a market for local produce and injecting money into the economy of the region. In times of hardship, the Army provided indispensable relief.[59]

When Major Smith arrived at Fort Stanton in May 1863, he found the post short of subsistence stores. The garrison had exhausted the supply of staples, including coffee, sugar and salt. Smith purchased provisions from the local citizens, providing a market for some of their produce when transporting it to a distant market was impractical. In July, Smith learned that local inhabitants needed food. He issued flour in small quantities to the needy settlers and wrote to headquarters for permission to issue more. He pointed out that these people were hard-working citizens who had money but nowhere to purchase their needs. Fighting in the area had destroyed trade and no merchants could be found. Carleton promptly granted permission and later sent specific orders regarding the issue of subsistence to civilians.[60]

In 1864, the post commander began hiring civilian employees to help repair the fort and perform such tasks as tending the post herd. This freed troops for more military duties, attracted tradesmen to the area, and brought money into the local economy. The number of employees and mixture of trades varied from month to month. In April the post employed eleven people and paid $315 in wages. September represented a low for the year of eight employees and $235 in wages. In December the payroll reached a high with fourteen people receiving $495 in wages. At various times the trades employed included carpenters, blacksmiths, wagon masters, hostlers, cobblers, guides, herders, and teamsters. The 1864 civilian payroll at Fort Stanton put more than $3000 into the local economy and brought much-needed tradesmen into the area. The employment of civilians at the fort continued in 1865, including the balance of an effort to repair the post, begun in October 1864, which included $3000 in material purchases.[61]

Near the end of 1863, hostile Indian activities slacked off, and soldiers at Fort Stanton had time to improve springs and make repairs to the fort. But their troubles with Indians were far from over. Indian raids were a persistent nuisance and the post had scouts in the field constantly, usually with little or no results beyond exhausting the troops and horses and wearing out their shoes. The problem was aggravated as Mescaleros began deserting the Bosque Redondo reservation in increasing numbers in September of 1863. By November 1865, virtually all the Indians had left the reservation and returned to their homelands.[62]

The Army made no plans for returning the Mescaleros to Bosque Redondo, leaving the garrison at Fort Stanton with the difficult task of pacifying them. When pursued, the Indians simply dispersed, fading into the mountains. In one incident, a small band of Indians stole four horses and four cattle from a ranch, retreating toward the Guadalupe Mountains. Capt. Charles M. Hubbell lead a detail from Fort Stanton in pursuit. He followed the raiders' trail until they scattered, then followed one trail until he lost it in rocky terrain. Hubbell spent an entire day searching for the trail before marching toward Dog Canyon and spending one night near San Augustine Spring. Finding no Indians in Dog Canyon, Hubbell returned to the post by way of the Rio Tularosa.

Hubbell's command marched about 200 miles and the rocky terrain wrecked the men's shoes. At Tularosa, Hubbell camped an extra day so his men could repair their shoes—many of the men's feet had been pierced by prickly pear spines. For the last five days of the scout Hubbell was obliged to mount some of his men on mules because of their exhausted condition.[63]

The return of the Mescaleros and the Army's difficulties in catching and punishing hostile Indians spawned rumors. In March 1865, one rumor had the Army abandoning Fort Stanton. This caused panic and General Carleton instructed Capt. William Brady, commanding Fort Stanton, to inform all residents along the Bonito, Ruidoso, and Tularosa rivers that two companies would be at Fort Stanton throughout the summer and that at least one additional company would be sent there for the winter. He was to advise the people to plant all the crops they could that spring. Dissatisfied with the progress of efforts to subdue the Mescaleros, Carleton concluded his letter by pointing out rather strongly that Brady and his troops were to pursue any Indians they saw, stating that the troops were not there to stand by and "...eat rations without doing any service in the way of killing hostile Indians."[64]

The troops at Fort Stanton were not simply sitting around eating rations. News of the reactivation of Fort Stanton, coupled with Carleton's and Carson's broad propaganda campaign, had attracted a significant number of farmers, ranchers, and prospectors to the region. The influx of settlers provided a plethora of easy prey for Indian raiders and continued depredations kept the troops at the fort constantly on scouts or in pursuit. At the end of 1865, the garrison at Fort Stanton was still hard put to deal with the bands of Indians whose raiding impeded the flow of immigrants to the area.[65]

Notes to Chapter II

1. Utley, *Frontiersmen in Blue*, p. 174; Wilson, *Merchants, Guns and Money*, p. 4; Frazer, pp. 181–82.

2. *Fort Stanton Returns*, roll 1216, post returns, February, May, June, 1861; Roberts to AAAG, Santa Fe, June 22, 1861, Roberts to AAAG, Santa Fe, June 24, 1861 (two letters), *Letters Received, Dept. of NM*, roll 14, R39, R37, R38.

3. Baylor to Washington, Sept. 21, 1861, *Official Records*, series 1, vol. 4, pp. 17–20; *Mesilla Times*, June 23, 1861, reprinted in the *Los Angeles Star*, Aug. 3, 1861; Lane, pp. 105–06, 108–15; Morris to Canby, June 25, 1861, *Letters Received, Dept. of NM*, roll 28, unregistered; *Mesilla Times*, June 30, 1865 and July 7, 1861, reprinted in the New Orleans *Daily Picayune* Aug. 6, 1861; Darlis A. Miller, "General James Henry Carleton in New Mexico", (Master's thesis, New Mexico State University, 1970), pp. 5–6; *Mesilla Times*, August 17, 1861 and August 29, 1861, extra issue.

4. Capt. J. H. Potter, July 27, 1861, Recapitulation of troops Surrendered at San Augustine Springs, N. Mex., Lt. Col. John R. Baylor, August 3, 1861, Report of Skirmish at Mesilla and Surrender of Union Troops at San Augustine Springs, and Baylor to Washington Sept. 21, 1861, *Official Records*, series 1, vol. 4, pp. 15, 16–20; Stanley, *Fort Stanton*, pp. 7, 18–21; Lane, pp. 109–14; John P. Wilson, "Whiskey at Fort Fillmore: A Story of the Civil War", *New Mexico Historical Review*, 68: (April, 1993) 121, 122–23, 127.

5. Ibid.

6. Roberts to Canby, July 7, Roberts to Anderson, Aug. 21, 1861, *Letters Received, Dept. of NM*, roll 28, unregistered; Roberts to Canby, Aug. 2, and Canby to AAG, U.S. Army, Aug. 4, 1861, *Official Records*, series 1, vol. 4, pp. 22, 2; Stanley, *Fort Stanton*, pp. 18–20.

7. Baylor to Van Dorn, Sept. 21, 1861, *Official Records*, series 1, vol. 4, pp. 19–20; *Mesilla Times*, Aug. 10, 1861, reprinted in the New Orleans *Daily Picayune* Sept. 5, 1861; Stanley, *Fort Stanton*, pp. 20–21; Wilson, *Merchants, Guns and Money*, pp. 14–15.

8. Baylor to Washington, Sept. 21, 1861, Pulliam to Baylor, Aug. 25 [?], 1861, and Baylor to Van Dorn, Aug. 14, 1861, *Official Records*, series 1, vol. 4, pp. 17–20, 24–25, 22–23; Stanley, *Fort Stanton*, pp. 20–21.

9. Stanley, *Fort Stanton*, p. 24; Baylor to Washington, Sept. 21, 1861, Proclamation to the People of Arizona from John R. Baylor, and Baylor to Van Dorn, Aug. 14, 1861, *Official Records*, series 1, vol. 4, pp. 17–20, 20–22, 22–23.

10. *Mesilla Times*, June 30, July 29, August 3, 10, 17, 1861: Utley, *Frontiersmen in Blue*, p. 235.

11. Wilson, Merchants, Guns and Money, p. 15–16; Moore to AAAG, Santa Fe, Sept. 29, 1861, *Letters Received*, roll 14, M83; Utley, *Frontiersmen in Blue*, p. 235.

12. *Mesilla Times*, Aug. 3, 17, 1861; Pulliam to Baylor, August 25 [?], *Official Records*, series 1, vol. 4, pp. 24–25; Frazer, pp. 181, 182; Wilson, p. 15.

13. Ibid.; Baylor to Van Dorn, Aug. 25, 1861, Baylor to Van Dorn, Aug. [?], 1861, Baylor to Van Dorn, Sept. [October] 1, 1861, and Chapin to Moore, Sept. 21, 1861, *Official Records*, series 1, vol. 4, pp. 24, 25–26, 30, 70–71; Frazer, p. 182; Stanley, *Fort Stanton*, pp. 22–23; Hays, p. 22.

14. Robert M. Utley, *Fort Union National Monument* (Wash., DC: National Park Service, U.S. Department of the Interior, 1962), pp. 26–31; *Letters Received, Dept. of NM*, roll 1, p. 2 of introduction.

15. Thelma S. Guild and Harvey L. Carter, *Kit Carson: A Pattern for Heroes* (Lincoln: University of Nebraska Press, 1984), p. 224; Miller, "General James Henry Carleton," pp. 35–36.

16. Ibid; Carleton to Thomas, Sept. 30, 1862, *Official Records*, series 1, vol. 15, pp. 576–77; Miller, "General James Henry Carleton", pp. 54, 55; Utley, *Fort Union*, p. 37.

17. Ibid;

18. Berney to Garrison, Oct. 31, 1862, *Letters Sent by Assistant Commissary of Subsistence Berney, Ft. Stanton New Mexico Only, Oct. 1862–May 1863* (NARS) RG 393, microfilm copy at New Mexico State University Library (hereafter referred to as *CSFS*); Carson to Cutler, Oct. 30, 1862, and Morrison to Cutler, Oct. 24, 1862, *Letters Received, Dept. of NM*, roll 15, C493, roll 17, M257; Guild and

Carter, p. 225; Darlis A. Miller, *Soldiers and Settlers: Military Supply in the Southwest, 1861–1885* (Albuquerque: University of New Mexico Press, 1989), p. 219.

19. Carson to Cutler, Oct 17, and Carson to Cutler, Oct 30, 1861, *Letters Received, Dept of NM*, roll 15, C521, C493.

20. Carleton to Thomas, Sept. 30, 1863, *Official Records*, series 1, vol. 15, pp. 576–77; Wilson, *Merchants, Guns and Money*, p. 16; Berney to Garrison, May 31, Berney to Garrison, Nov. 10, and Berney to Garrison, Nov. 22, 1862, *CSFS*; *Santa Fe Weekly Gazette*, Nov. 15, 1862; Carleton to Doolittle, Oct. 23, 1863, Senate Report Number 156, "Condition of Indian Tribes," 39th Congress, 2nd Session (hereafter referred to as SR 156), p. 98; Miller, *Soldiers and Settlers*, pp. 60–61.

21. Carson to Cutler, Oct. 30, 1862, *Letters Received, Dept. of NM*, roll 15, C493; Carleton to Thomas, Sept. 30, and Carleton to Carson, Oct. 12, 1862, *Official Records*, series 1, vol. 15, pp. 576–77, 579.

22. Guild and Carter, pp. 225–26; Carleton to Carson, Oct. 12, 1862, *Official Records*, series 1, Vol. 15, p. 579.

23. Carleton to DeForrest, Sept. 26, and Cutler to Commanding Officer, Fort Stanton, Sept. 14, 1864, *Official Records*, series 1, vol 41, part 3, pp. 399–400, 196; Carleton to Thomas, Feb. 1, 1863, *Official Records*, series 1, vol. 15, pp. 669–70.

24. Carleton to Carson, Oct. 12, Carleton to West, Oct. 11, and West to McCleave, Nov. 14, 1862, *Official Records*, series 1, vol. 15, pp. 579, 580–81, 596–97; Miller, "General James Henry Carleton", p. 36.

25. Ibid.; Carleton to West, Oct. 14, 1862, *Letters Sent*, roll 3, vol. 9, #890; Carleton to West, Oct 11, 1862, *Official Records*, Series 1, vol. 15, pp. 580–81; Carleton to West, Oct 3, Carleton to West, Oct 14, and Carleton to West, Nov 10, 1862, *Letters Sent*, roll 3, vol 9, #836, #890, #996.

26. Morrison to Cutler, October 24, Carson to Cutler, Oct. 30, and Carson to Cutler, Nov. 12, 1862, *Letters Received, Dept. of NM*, roll 17, M257, roll 15, C493, C518; Guild and Carter, p. 226; Lawrence C. Kelly, *Navajo Roundup: Selected Correspondence of Kit Carson's Expedition Against the Navajo, 1863–1865* (Boulder, CO: The Pruett Publishing Company, 1970) pp. 12–15; Utley, *Frontiersmen in Blue*, p. 236; *Santa Fe Weekly Gazette*, Nov. 15, 29,

1862; James E. Farmer, *My Life With the Army in the West: Memoirs of James E. Farmer, 1858–1898,* Dale F. Giese, ed. (Santa Fe: Stagecoach Press, 1967; repr., Silver City, NM: Dale F. Giese, 1993) pp. 49–51; Guild and Carter, pp. 226–27.

27. Ibid.; Kelly, p. 14; *Santa Fe Weekly Gazette,* Nov. 8, 15, 1862; Carson to Cutler, Dec. 9, and Carson to Cutler, Nov. 12, 1862, *Letters Received, Dept. of NM,* roll 15, C518, C532.

28. Hays, p. 28; Farmer, pp. 49–50; Utley, *Frontiersmen in Blue,* p. 236; *Santa Fe Gazette,* Nov. 8, 15, 1862; Carleton to West, Oct. 11, 1862, *Official Records,* series 1, vol. 15, pp. 580–81; Carleton to Updegraph, Apr. 10, 1863, SR 156, p. 107.

29. Morrison to Cutler, Oct. 24, Morrison to Cutler, Nov. 22, Morrison to Cutler, Nov 24, Carson to Cutler, Oct. 30 and Carson to Cutler, Nov. 12, 1862, *Letters Received, Dept. of NM,* roll 17, M257, M273, M274, roll 15, C493, C518; *Santa Fe Weekly Gazette,* Nov. 29, 1862; Miller, "General James Henry Carleton," p. 61; Guild and Carter, p. 226; Kelly R. Hays, "Fort Stanton, A History of its Relationship with the Mescalero Apaches" (Master's thesis, New Mexico State University, 1988) pp. 28–29; Dale F. Giese, *Forts of New Mexico: Echoes of the Bugle,* (Silver City, n.p., pp. 29–30.

30. Carson to Carleton, Dec. 14 and Carson to Cutler, Dec. 24, 1862, *Letters Received, Dept. of NM,* roll 15, C534, roll 18, C6.

31. Carson to Cutler, Dec. 24, 1862, Carson to Cutler, Jan 4, and Carson to Cutler, Jan. 17, 1863, *Letters Received, Dept. of NM,* roll 18, C6, C24, C33.

32. Carson to Cutler, Jan. 4, 1863, *Letters Received, Dept. of NM,* roll 18, C24.

33. Carleton to Cutler, undated, *Santa Fe Weekly Gazette,* Dec. 27, 1862.

34. *Santa Fe Weekly Gazette,* Dec. 27, 1862.

35. Carleton to Thomas, Feb. 1, 1863, *Official Records,* series 1, vol. 15, pp. 669–70; Miller, "General James Henry Carleton", p. 62.

36. Guild and Carter, pp. 228–29.

37. Kelly, pp. 15–16; Guild and Carter, pp. 228–29; *Fort Stanton Returns,* roll 1216, post returns, March, May, 1863.

38. Carleton to Thomas, Mar. 19, 1863, SR 156, p. 106; Carleton to Thomas, Apr. 12, Carleton to Lamy, June 12, 1863, SR 156, pp. 108–109, 112; Kelly, p. 17.

39. Meyers, pp. 21–22; Guild and Carter, p. 226; Kelly, p. 15.

40. Carleton to Halleck, May 10, 1863, SR 156, p. 110;

41. Meyers, p. 22; Utley, *Frontiersmen in Blue*, pp. 236–37; Miller, *Soldiers and Settlers*, pp. 60–61; Wilson, *Merchants, Guns and Money*, p. 19.

42. Hays, p. 37.

43. *Fort Stanton Returns*, roll 1216, post returns, March, 1863; Carleton to Commanding Officer, Fort Stanton, Apr. 10, 1863, SR 156, p. 107.

44. Ibid.

45. Hays, p. 39; Abreu to Cutler, Mar. 27, 1863, *Letters Received, Dept. of NM*, roll 18, A48; General Orders No. 3, Department of New Mexico, *Official Records*, Series 1, vol. 15, pp. 227–30; *Fort Stanton Returns*, roll 1216, post returns, Mar.–Apr., 1863.

46. Abreu to Smith, May 11, and Smith to Cutler, May 7, 1863, *Letters Received, Dept. of NM*, roll 20, S89 with enclosure, S82.

47. Smith to Cutler, May 20, 1863, *Letters Received, Dept. of NM*, roll 20, S97.

48. Ibid; Hays, pp. 40–41; *Fort Stanton Returns*, roll 1216, post returns, May, June, 1863.

49. Cutler to Smith, June 27, 1863, SR 156, p. 118–19; Smith to Cutler, June 24, and Smith to Cutler, June 27, 1863, *Letters Received, Dept. of NM*, roll 20, S119, S118.

50. Cutler to Smith, June 27, and Carleton to Smith, July 2, 1863, SR 156, pp. 118–20; Abreu to Cutler, Mar. 27, Smith to Cutler, June 24, and Smith to Cutler, June 27, 1863, *Letters Received, Dept. of NM*, roll 18, A48, and roll 20, S119, S118; General Orders number 3, Department of New Mexico, *Official Records*, pp. 228–31; Hays, pp. 40–41.

51. Carleton to Smith, July 2, 1863, SR 156, pp. 119–20; Smith to Cutler, July 17, 1863, *Letters Received, Dept. of NM*, roll 20, S138.

52. Carleton to Smith, July 2, Carleton to Smith July 29, and Carleton to Smith, Aug. 7, 1863, SR 156, pp. 119–21, 125; *Fort Stanton Returns*, roll 1216, post return, July, 1863; Smith to Cutler, July 17, Smith to Cutler, July 24, and Smith to Cutler, Aug 7, 1863, *Letters Received, Dept. of NM*, roll 20, S138, S142, S158, enclosure; Miller, "General James Henry Carleton", pp. 75–76.

53. Carleton to Smith, July 29, 1863, SR 156, pp. 120–21; *Fort Stanton Returns*, roll 1216, post returns, July–Aug., 1863.

54. *Fort Stanton Returns*, roll 1216, post returns, Aug. 1863; Carleton to Smith, July 29, 1863, SR 156, pp. 120–21; Hays, pp. 47–48.

55. *Fort Stanton Returns*, roll 1216, post returns, Aug.–Oct, 1863; Smith to Cutler, Sept. 7, Smith to Cutler, Sept. 10, and Smith to Cutler, Sept. 23, 1863, *Letters Received, Dept. of NM*, roll 20, S191, with enclosures, S189, S209; Carleton to Smith, Sept. 18, 1863, *Letters Sent*, roll 3, vol. 10, #991.

56. Hollister to Cutler, Sept. 27, 1863, *Letters Received, Dept. of NM*, roll 20, S227.
Note: This report was either an inclusion in a letter from Smith to Cutler or was misfiled. Either way, it is filed as a separate letter on roll 20.

57. Smith to Cutler, Sept. 23, Smith to Cutler, Oct. 1, Smith to Cutler, Oct 4, and Hollister to Cutler, Sept. 27, 1863, *Letters Received, Dept. of NM*, roll 20, S209, S210, S223, S227; *Fort Stanton Returns*, roll 1216, post returns, Sept.– Nov., 1863.

58. Smith to Cutler, Oct. 4, 1863, *Letters Received Dept. of NM*, roll 20, S223; The Santa Fe *New Mexican*, April 25, 1863.

59. Wilson, *Merchants, Guns and Money*, pp. 20, 24; Miller, "General James Henry Carleton", pp. 64, 71–72; Smith to Cutler, Oct. 4, 1863, *Letters Received Dept. of NM*, roll 20, S223; The Santa Fe *New Mexican*, April 25, 1863.

60. Smith to Cutler, May 29, Smith to Cutler, July 30, Smith to Cutler, Aug. 5, and Smith to Cutler, Aug. 14, 1863, *Letters Received, Dept. of NM*, roll 20, S100, S150, S156, S164; DeForest to Smith, Aug. 5, 1863, *Letters Sent*, roll 3, vol. 9, #757; Hays, p. 39.

61. *Fort Stanton Returns*, roll 1216, post returns, Apr.–Dec., 1864; Seckler and Hosmer, p. 29; Miller, *Soldiers and Settlers*, p. 220.

62. *Fort Stanton Returns,* roll 1216, post returns, 1864–65; Hays, pp. 53, 55–56; Miller, *Soldiers and Settlers,* p. 61.

63. Hays, p. 55; *Fort Stanton Returns,* roll 1216, post returns, Mar.–May, 1865; Hubbell to Brady, April 26, 1865, *Letters Received, Dept. of NM,* roll 27, H57.

64. Carleton to Brady, Apr. 30, 1865, *Letters Received, Fort Stanton, RG 98, Letters Received and Sent, Forts Garland, Conrad, Craig, Stanton, Union,* (NARS) microfilm copy at New Mexico State Archives and records Center, Santa Fe (hereafter referred to as *Letters Received, Fort Stanton*).

65. Miller, *Soldiers and Settlers,* pp. 60–61.

Chapter III

MAKING THE REGION SAFE
FOR SETTLEMENT

Despite the successful Indian campaigns of 1863–64, Indians still raided at will in the Ruidoso, Bonito, and Peñasco river valleys. The Fort Stanton garrison was constantly in pursuit of raiders or scouting for Indian camps. Following the Civil War, westward migration increased, but Indian activity around Fort Stanton reduced the impact to the region. The Army's job was to protect settlers, but troops unfamiliar with the area were unable to catch and punish the hostile Indians. It would take more than five years for the troops at Fort Stanton to establish a commanding presence in the region.

Small groups of Mescalero Apaches began leaving Bosque Redondo in the Fall of 1863, as the first Navajos began arriving. In early November 1865, the remaining Mescaleros, except for a handful who were old and sick, left the reservation, many of them seeking refuge in the Sacramento Mountains and Sierra Blancas. The Army did not pursue them and had no immediate plans to deal with them.[1]

By June 1865 a flood of escaped Apaches and Navajos passed through, or encamped in, the region around Fort Stanton. The garrison tried to cope with a situation reminiscent of the 1850s, when Fort Stanton troops were kept busy chasing bands of Indians who had committed depredations, usually with little or no results.[2] On June 16, 1865, Capt. William Brady, commanding Fort Stanton, received word that Lt. Edwin J. Edger's command, camped about forty miles from the post on the Rio Bonito, was surrounded by Indians and in peril of losing its horses. Brady saddled all the horses he had, sixteen, and took a party to reinforce Edger. Upon his arrival, Brady found the Indians had fled. Taking Edger's command with him Brady scouted the Capitan Mountains, finding no sign of the Indians. He then sent Edger's detail through Carrizo Canyon while he returned to the fort to have his horses shod. On June 20 Brady learned that Maj. Emil Fritz had passed nearby in pursuit of 500 Navajos who had escaped from Fort Sumner on June 17.[3]

On June 21 Brady received reports of Indian activity at Gallinas Spring. He began pursuit and sent orders to Edger to join him at Patos Spring. When he reached Patos Spring, Brady encountered a detachment of New Mexico Volunteers that had been pursuing a large band of Navajos from Gallinas Spring. The volunteers' horses were exhausted. He directed these men to rest at Patos Spring and took his detail in pursuit of the Indians. Brady was obliged to encamp when he reached Largo Canyon because his horses, having traveled over 200 miles in five days, were spent. On June 22, Edger joined Brady, but his horses were jaded and several had collapsed. Brady sent several details to scout the trails on foot in hope of picking up fresh tracks. The next day, on the Albuquerque Road, Brady's force took up the trail of a band of Indians that was being pursued by a cavalry company. Brady followed this trail for two days into the Oscura Mountains. Here the troops saw some Indians on foot but were unable to catch them because the men and horses were exhausted and had been without water for nearly two days.[4]

After finding water and refreshing his command, Brady took up the pursuit and encountered Major Fritz's trail, with evidence that a large band of Navajos was in hot pursuit of Fritz. Brady gave chase along this trail for more than twelve miles before the Indians dispersed, leaving him only Fritz's trail to follow. That night a scout, sent out by Brady to determine what the Indians were doing, informed him that they had regrouped and were headed for the San Andres Mountains. The following day Brady gave up the chase, going to the Rio Grande to water and rest his exhausted command. His men's shoes, clothing, and horses were worn out completely. On June 26, Brady left his troops at San Pedro under the command of Capt. Peter Bishop while he went to Fort Craig and arranged to refit his command. Bishop was to bring the horses to Fort Craig the next day. Brady had been accompanied by four-teen Hispano citizens whom he recommended be compensated for six days service. After leaving Fort Craig, Brady continued his pursuit and eventually came to Las Cruces, where he remained a full week before leaving for Fort Stanton on July 12. Brady arrived at Fort Stanton on July 16, his horses and men were in poor condition.[5] In all this exhaust-ing pursuit, Brady succeeded only in wearing out his horses and men and taking a five-year-old Mescalero boy, abandoned by the Indians during the chase, to Fort Craig.[6]

Controlling the Indians was not the only problem reminiscent of the 1850s. Operations were severely hampered by a shortage of men and supplies. From January through September 1865, the garrison at Fort Stanton consisted of Companies A and H, 1st Cavalry, New Mexico Volunteers. In October Companies D and E replaced Companies A and H. Fort Stanton was again a two-company post, with an aggregate compliment of 150 to 160 men. This figure included personnel absent on detached service, men on leave, transients, and those sick in the hospital. The effective force was usually under 100 men. In July, Captain Brady reported that his command had eighty men for duty, all extremely fatigued, and all of his horses were unfit for service. The rifles his men had could not be fired while mounted. This was a decided disadvantage because Indians rarely made a stand. In a pursuit or run-ning fight the rifles were of little use. In September, Brady complained that he needed two full companies of cavalry. He had no first sergeant, nor any enlisted men capable of performing the duties of clerk.[7]

Getting supplies was a vexing problem that seemed never to be solved. Not only could the post not get suitable arms, but basic staples were scarce and the mail was often late for reasons other than hostile Indians. In August 1867, the mail was delayed a week at Fort Sumner for no apparent reason. In September, Lt. Gerald Russell, commanding the post, complained that needed supplies, ordered by Headquarters in Santa Fe from Fort Union nearly two months earlier, had not yet arrived. The post was completely out of candles, soap, sugar, salt, and vinegar. Russell was unable to get any of these supplies locally and urgently requested that a small supply be sent as soon as possible.[8] Problems associated with the shortage of supplies exacerbated the primitive living conditions at the post. In the 1850s the troops at Fort Stanton resided in a comfortable and sturdy fort. During the Civil War the post was burned and looted, leaving the post-war garrison stationed at one of the most primitive posts in New Mexico.[9]

Although a substantial garrison had been stationed at Fort Stanton since October 1862, little effort had been made to repair the damage wrought when the post was abandoned and burned. The post was in poor condition and only a few of the original stone buildings were still inhabitable. The sick were housed in the ruins of what had been the original hospital. All the buildings leaked badly during heavy rains, and rubble lay where it had fallen four years before. In October 1864, Maj. Herbert M. Enos, Division Quartermaster and Special Inspector for the Department of New Mexico, visited Fort Stanton briefly. Upon his return to Santa Fe, Enos recommended that the post either be rebuilt or abandoned. General Carleton allotted $3,000 for materials to repair the fort, with the labor to be provided by the soldiers at the post. The effort was not successful. The funds were inadequate and the labor of the busy soldiers was insufficient.[10]

In the Spring of 1865, following the Civil War, the United States Army reorganized. The chain of command included the Division as the largest unit. Each Division had several Departments and each Department had several Districts. In June, the Army reduced New Mexico from a department to a district and assigned it to the Department of California. In September, the District of New Mexico replaced the Department of New Mexico. In October, the Army transferred the District of New Mexico to the Department of Missouri, which was headquartered in Chicago under the command of Gen. Philip Sheridan. The District of New Mexico remained a district of the Department of Missouri until November 1880, when the Army moved it to the newly created Department of Arizona. The District of New Mexico remained in the Department of Arizona until the Army abolished it, in August 1890.[11]

In 1868, the District of New Mexico allocated $20,000 for the refurbishment of Fort Stanton. The money was intended for use in repairing the old stone buildings and building new ones. The post quartermaster awarded contracts in July to Lawrence G. Murphy for 200,000 board feet of lumber at a total cost of $9,390, and to Henry

C. Harrison for 500,000 wooden shingles at a total cost of $4,490. In 1867, after mustering out of the Army, Murphy and Emil Fritz, who had both formerly commanded Fort Stanton, formed a partnership, Lawrence G. Murphy and Company (L. G. Murphy & Co.), and opened a store at the post. They bought out L. B. Maxwell, post trader since 1863, and took over his business.[12]

The refurbishment effort attracted a significant number of workers to the area and infused a substantial amount of money into the region's economy. Civilian employment at Fort Stanton, in March 1868, consisted of one guide being paid $45 per month. In April, the number of civilian employees jumped to twenty-five with a payroll of $1,130. In May, civilian employment climbed to sixty-two and in September the fort employed 105 persons, paying $4,739 in wages. In October, the number of employees dropped to 101 but the wages paid rose to $4,968. The payroll reached a peak in January 1869, when the post paid $5,734 to 109 employees. Between April 1 1868 and April 1 1869, the Quartermaster Department at Fort Stanton paid $47,689 in wages to civilian workers and the Commissary Department paid another $150.[13]

General Philip Sheridan, commanding the Department of Missouri, startled by the cost of renovations at the post, ordered expenditures to be reduced. After January 1869, the number of employees and total wages paid declined steadily until June 30, when the entire effort was suspended. Interestingly, in February, the Adjutant for Commissary Stores (ACS) hired a clerk for the Commissary Department, a job normally filled by an enlisted man. The clerk remained on the payroll until the end of June. Apparently the ACS, Lt. William Gerlach, saved someone's job in the wake of Sheridan's order to cut back. The post had twenty-eight employees on per diem, which often included a ration or portion thereof. Managing this added responsibility may have required an additional clerk's services. However, Army policy was to record such rations in post returns as part of a person's pay (i.e. 1 painter @ $2.75 per day and 1 ration.) No such entries, for any employees, appear in the post returns for that period. It is entirely possible, of course, that Gerlach could not find an enlisted man competent to act as clerk during that time. Gerlach later complained that uncertain tenure was a substantial barrier to obtaining employees. By July the post employed one clerk, one wagonmaster, and one guide. Wages paid amounted to only $228. However, in the three months from April 1 to July 1, Fort Stanton had paid $12,800 in wages to civilian workers. When the post renovation effort halted, the project had injected about $75,000 in wages and material purchases into the economy of Lincoln County.[14]

Renovation efforts at the post did not remain halted long. When Ltc. August V. Kautz took command of the post in October, he was not satisfied with the state of repairs. The new stone buildings for the officers and men were not completed and the sick were still housed in the ruins of the original hospital. One carpenter had been employed at the fort since August, but that was far too little to have any significant impact. Kautz argued that if the building materials accumulated at the post were allowed to sit unused for a long period, they would rot, constituting a great financial loss to the government. The district commander authorized Kautz to resume renovation efforts and, in March 1870, the post employed two more carpenters and a mason. By May, the fort employed twelve civilians. Although expenditures for labor never again reached the proportions of the earlier effort, peaking at $1,097 in October, work on the post continued steadily until the renovation was completed in November 1871. During that time 12 civilians, on average, worked at the post and the Army paid $18,403 in wages to residents of Lincoln County.[15]

In less than four years the Fort Stanton Quartermaster and Commissary Departments paid $107,283 locally in wages alone. Fort Stanton was in an isolated area and, although many of the workers may have saved the majority of their wages, most of them spent a significant portion of their earnings within the area on food, housing, and other necessities.[16] Lincoln, the nearest population center to the post, undoubtedly benefited greatly from this boon. In 1860, real estate holdings in Lincoln amounted to $25,775 and most of this property was abandoned during the Civil War. Real estate holdings in Lincoln had risen to $75,770 by 1870, including $1000 in real estate held by the Fort Stanton post surgeon.[17]

When General Garland established Fort Stanton in 1855, La Placita del Rio Bonito (Lincoln), did not appear in the census records. The 1860 and 1870 censuses listed it as Rio Bonito. It was known as La Placita, or Placita, to the locals and the military at Fort Stanton. By

1860 Rio Bonito, or Placita, was a fairly prosperous town. In 1869, the state legislature divided Socorro County, forming two counties. The western half remained Socorro County while the eastern half became Lincoln County. In December, the legislature designated Rio Bonito as the county seat of Lincoln County and officially changed the town's name to Lincoln. However, official records continued to refer to the town as Placita. In 1873, the Postal Service established a post office in Lincoln and the town began using the name Lincoln, probably as the result of a post office order. By 1870, before the refurbishment of Fort Stanton was completed, real estate holdings had nearly tripled the 1860 figures.[18]

Reconstruction work at the post did more than inject money into the region's economy; it attracted skilled labor to the area. While the principal occupation in the region in 1870 was farming, carpenters, masons, teamsters, blacksmiths, shoemakers, and other skilled tradesmen lived in or near Lincoln. The only seamstress, the wife of a soldier, lived at the fort. Although most of these tradesmen were Anglo, many were Hispanic. Nearly all of the trades reported by residents of Lincoln in 1870 represented skills employed at the fort. More tradesmen lived in Lincoln than worked at the post. In March 1870, only one mason worked at the fort, but four lived in Lincoln. While some of the skilled people employed at Fort Stanton in 1870 probably left the region when the renovations were completed, many remained.[19]

The town of Rio Bonito, Lincoln after 1869, had an unusual population makeup. Remote towns in New Mexico tended to be entirely Hispanic. However, both Hispanos and Anglos lived in Rio Bonito. In 1860 the population of Rio Bonito was 257, including 36 families. Seventy percent of the population was Hispanic; the rest was Anglo. Some of the Hispanics, who fled when Fort Stanton was abandoned in 1861, went to Manzano. Two years later Manzano residents were in a desperate situation as the crops had failed repeatedly. In December 1863, John A. Clark, Surveyor General of New Mexico, reported that the heads of at least eighty Hispanic families intended to move to the Rio Bonito Valley. Between 1863 and 1870 Hispanos settled along the Rio Bonito while Anglos preferred to settle along the Ruidoso and Hondo Rivers. The area was virtually depopulated in 1861, when Fort Stanton was abandoned, but the population grew rapidly after Christopher Carson reopened the fort and declared the area safe for settlement in 1863. In 1864, Hispanics from other locations within New Mexico migrated to the Rio Bonito Valley. In 1866, Maj. Lawrence G. Murphy, commanding Fort Stanton, reported the population along the Bonito, Ruidoso, and Hondo rivers as 425, 89% of whom were Hispanic. Between 1866 and 1870 the Anglo population more than doubled. By 1870 the population of Lincoln was 510, including 123 Anglos and more than 200 families. Hispanos made up 76% of the total population.[20]

Like the tradesmen, former soldiers who had served at Fort Stanton often settled in the area. Soldiers serving in Southwestern posts saw the various regions first hand. This experience enabled them to make informed decisions about where they would settle upon leaving the Army.[21] Paul Dowlin, who owned a mill with his brother William, commanded Fort Stanton in 1865. Lawrence Murphy and Emil Fritz, prominent citizens of Lincoln in the 1870s, served at the post. William Brady, who once commanded Fort Stanton, took the census in Lincoln County in 1870, listing himself as a farmer living in Lincoln. Saturnino Baca, formerly a captain in the New Mexico Volunteers, also resided in Lincoln. Pvt. Frank Lesnett, discharged at Fort Stanton in 1875, went to Chicago to marry Elizabeth Cavenaugh and then brought her to Ruidoso where he later acquired Dowlin's Mill.[22] In 1870 the ethnic makeup of the Anglo population of Lincoln closely resembled that of the garrison at Fort Stanton. Particularly represented, in order of numbers present, were the United States, Ireland, Germany, Great Britain, and Western Europe.[23]

While the settlements surrounding Fort Stanton grew and prospered, the soldiers at the post, and throughout southern New Mexico, experienced great difficulty in controlling hostile Indians. Between the end of the Civil War and the Spring of 1869, the posts of southern New Mexico reported only thirty-three fights with Indians compared with 137 engagements reported in Arizona. Until the troops could consistently overtake and punish raiders, the Indian troubles would continue. The Indians were familiar with the region, while the soldiers were not. The Indians also carried water in large animal skins, often with a capacity of several gallons, while the troops carried only one quart, and therefore had to stop more often. Pursuing troops, unfamiliar with the region, were obliged to use the same water supply their enemy had used. Knowing this, the Indians took all the water or attempted to render it undrinkable before they moved on. During a lengthy pursuit in June 1865, Captain Brady's quarry plugged springs and fouled water holes so his men and horses could not use them. Knowing the country enabled the Indians to travel rapidly at night. Pursuing troops traveled more slowly, and had to travel during daylight, in order to follow the trail.[24]

Brady took steps to remedy at least part of the problem. He kept patrols of from twelve to twenty men in the field at all times. In addition to familiarizing the men with the region, Brady hoped the patrols would flush out hostile Indians and bring them to submission. This effort was not immediately successful, however. During July and August, Indians killed six men, a woman, and two boys in Lincoln. Brady did not have enough troops to mount more than one or two scouts at any one time. The Indians began attacking in small groups at several widely separated points at the same time, making pursuit almost impossible. In one incident Brady suspected a group from the Bosque Redondo reservation had committed depredations near Lincoln and returned to the reservation. He suggested that this group be rounded up and punished in the presence of the residents of that reservation as an object lesson. Reservation authorities chose not to do that.[25]

Maj. Emil Fritz took command of Fort Stanton in October 1865. Fritz, like Brady, energetically scouted the area, augmenting his scouts with armed civilian volunteers. Fritz expected the civilians, more familiar with the region than the soldiers, to improve the efficiency of the scouts, but they did not produce the results expected and morale at the fort began to fail. When a group of 73 local citizens, led by Juan Jose Romero, petitioned General Carleton for protection from Mescalero outrages in March 1866, Carleton dispatched Maj. Lawrence G. Murphy and one company of New Mexico Volunteer Cavalry to augment the garrison at Fort Stanton. Murphy arrived in April and took command of the post. Murphy believed that waiting for the Indians to act then chasing after them was ineffective. He adopted a preventive approach to the problem and kept three or four small groups of cavalry in the field as a deterrent. He also set out pickets in the Gallinas Mountains, La Luz, and Alamo canyon. This approach worked and the number of Mescalero raids diminished.[26]

In 1866, the volunteer troops were mustered out of the service, as part of the post-Civil War demobilization, and replaced with regulars. In August, Col. Paul Harwood of the 3rd U.S. Cavalry Regiment took command of Fort Stanton. Unlike the volunteer troops who had finally become familiar with the terrain, the regulars knew nothing of the region and Indian raids increased. In January 1867 Lt. Dean S. Monahan, now commanding the post, requested more troops. General Carleton responded that he must defend the area with the troops he had and the inhabitants of Tularosa, Ruidoso, and Lincoln would have to learn to defend their own settlements.[27] The citizens did try to defend themselves and recover stolen property, but they had limited success. Adding to the problem, when the settlers came to the fort for arms and ammunition, supplies were so short that the post commander was unable to provide them. In February 1868, Indians stole stock from a ranch near Fort Stanton. A group of citizens pursued the raiders and recovered the stolen stock but did not catch the thieves.[28]

By July 1867, the raids reached extreme proportions and New Mexico's territorial delegate to Congress, J. Francisco Chavez, recommended that the Mescaleros be forced onto a reservation south of Fort Stanton in the vicinity of Rio Felix. Lt. Gerald Russell received authorization from District Headquarters to hire guides and interpreters to locate the Mescaleros and arrange peace with them, setting up a reservation at an undesignated location near Fort Stanton. Residents in the vicinity of Fort Stanton paid three Hispanos and the post guide, a man named Ignacio, to seek out the Mescaleros and bring them in for talks. Lieutenant Russell provided the four men with fifteen days' rations. After fifteen days, the men returned without making any contact with the Mescaleros. Ignacio did recover a horse stolen from a local resident, but that was the only success. Neither the residents nor troops from Fort Stanton made any further attempts to contact the Mescaleros.[29]

The Mescalero raids in the region between the Pecos River and Fort Stanton continued throughout 1868. In March, Capt. Frank Stanwood, commanding Fort Stanton, established picket posts on the Rio Tularosa and Hondo Rivers and at the junction of the Bonito and Ruidoso Rivers. During the same month, the Mescaleros killed eleven men and two women and stole 2,000 sheep in Tularosa. The people of Tularosa came to Fort Stanton for arms and ammunition, but the post

76

commander had no weapons to spare. Meanwhile, the garrison at Fort Stanton, diligently scouting and pursuing hostile Indians, gained in skill and effectiveness. The turning point came in December 1869 when Lt. Howard B. Cushing led a scout into the Guadalupe Mountains and destroyed two large *rancherías*.[30]

Cushing, with thirty-five men of Company F, 3rd Cavalry, twenty-eight citizens, both Anglo and Hispano, and 2nd Lt. Franklin Yeaton, left Fort Stanton on December 19, 1869 carrying twenty days' provisions.[31] In the afternoon of December 26 the troops found ponies grazing on a hillside. Cushing sent a skirmish line up the hillside, with mounted parties on each flank. The troops came upon a *ranchería*, and promptly attacked. Although taken by surprise, the Indians rallied and resisted.[32]

After a brief but intense battle in which Lieutenant Yeaton was seriously wounded, the Indians scattered and fled. Unable to pursue on horseback because of the terrain, Cushing dismounted his men and pressed the pursuit on foot until his men were too tired to continue. A large number of Indians were killed and wounded and no effort was made to take prisoners. Returning to the camp, the troops burned between forty and fifty tents, 15,000 to 20,000 pounds of prepared Mescal, 15,000 pounds of jerked beef, a large number of buffalo robes, and tanned beef, deer, and antelope hides. The soldiers also destroyed cloths, weapons, cooking utensils, Indian liquor, and more riding saddles than could be counted. The *ranchería* was so large and well provisioned that it took several hours to destroy it. The burning camp set the grass and woods afire, forcing Cushing to move off about a mile before bivouacking for the night.[33]

The next day the troops headed back along the main trail toward home. On the return march the men saw a few Indians at great distances and Cushing observed smoke signals in the direction of the Guadalupe Mountains. On December 30, Cushing selected forty well-mounted men and sent the rest of the command to the Rio Peñasco. Taking the forty-man detail, Cushing headed for the southern point of the Guadalupe Mountains, marching hard and fast. In one of the canyons of the Guadalupes, Cushing discovered and attacked another large *ranchería*. After the Indians fled, the soldiers destroyed the camp and all its accouterments.[34]

The second *ranchería* was also well provisioned. Noting a large number of families in each lodge Cushing surmised that this camp included the refugees from his previous attack. The next day, January 1, 1870, Cushing lead his party to the Rio Peñasco where he joined the rest of his command and returned to Fort Stanton, arriving at the post on January 6, 1870. On this scout more than fifty horses and mules were captured. One horse was given to each of the civilian volunteers and five others were "...used up on the trip to save Government animals." On January 13, Col. August V. Kautz, commanding Fort Stanton, sent Cushing's report to Headquarters with a note on the jacket recommending Cushing and Yeaton for a brevet promotion of one grade for their actions on this scout.[35]

Cushing's punitive expedition severely hampered the Mescaleros' capacity to make war and, although it did not end hostilities, it demonstrated that the soldiers had learned how to catch and punish the Indians and served notice that raiding and pillaging was no longer profitable. Sometimes the civilian population seemed to be sending a different message to the Indians and the troops. On one occasion troops, responding to a report of Indians stealing cattle, were misinformed as to the time of the raid and the direction in which the thieves fled. The victims were uncooperative and seemed disinterested in recovering their cattle.[36] In another incident, the wagonmaster of a train loaded with goods for Fort Stanton seemed to have deliberately put his train in jeopardy. The men of the train, unarmed, camped in a conspicuous location and allowed the animals to graze unguarded. One warrior distracted the men of the train, who sought cover upon seeing him, while several other Indians made off with the goods and animals. Considerable time elapsed before someone notified the fort so that, when the soldiers arrived, the trail had vanished and they could not pursue the culprits. Capt. Chambers McKibbin, commanding the post, accused the wagonmaster of criminal carelessness.[37]

By the Spring of 1870, the constant Indian scouts had yielded another dividend. As the troops became more familiar with the area, they discovered better routes of travel. In May, Colonel Kautz reported a new road to Fort Union that reduced the traveling distance by more than fifty miles. The new road went from Fort Union to Sapello Creek, through Las Vegas by way of several springs and water holes to Fort Sumner. From there the road went to Hopkins' Ranch with stops at two

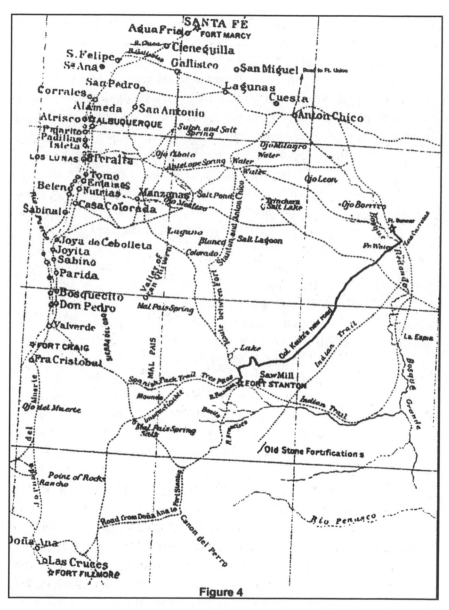

Figure 4

The shortcut road to Fort Sumner scouted and constructed by Colonel Kautz's troops in the spring of 1870. This road reduced the traveling distance to Fort Sumner by more than fifty miles. (Adapted from the *Atlas to Accompany the Official Records of the Union and Confederate Armies, 1861–1865*: Part I, plate 54, map 1) springs along the way. From Hopkins' Ranch it was a short distance to Fort Stanton. This road improved mail service and reduced the cost of shipping between Santa Fe and the towns of Tularosa and Lincoln, as well as Fort Stanton. Mail was delivered once a week before this new road was opened. New military roads fostered a steady improvement in communications and by 1878 mail arrived from Santa Fe and Roswell three times a week. Improved communications and the influx of settlers were significant factors in forcing the Mescaleros to make peace.[38]

By October 1871, the region was peaceful. From May through September Kautz, McKibbin, and Capt. William McCleave took turns commanding the post and leading scouts in the field. They kept from one to three small scouting parties at a time in the field and none of them reported any indications of trouble. Lt. Argus G. Hennisee, Indian agent for the Mescaleros, had been working to contact and conclude a treaty with the Mescaleros. In July, Cadette arrived with more than 300 Mescaleros to arrange peace. Agent Andrew J. Curtis, who replaced Hennisee, concluded an agreement with Cadette, who promised that more of his tribesmen would join him in the Fall. The need for scouting parties and demands for protection from troops at the fort diminished significantly, and the soldiers were kept busy with more mundane activities. In October, the garrison engaged primarily in escort duty, but by November few escorts were required. Except for minor incidents, Curtis' agreement prevailed for two years.[39]

During 1870 and 1871, as the Indian fighting subsided and communications improved, the importance of Fort Stanton diminished rapidly in the minds of some administrators. In 1870, Gen. John Pope, commanding the Department of the Missouri, believed Fort Stanton was no longer of any military value. He wanted to close the fort but Secretary of War William W. Belknap did not concur. Belknap agreed the post was militarily unnecessary, but believed it was vital to the community economically.[40] Belknap may have been partially influenced by personal concerns. His son had come to Fort Stanton for his health and was improving steadily under the care of the post surgeon.[41]

In May 1872, Congress enacted a bill reducing the size of the Fort Stanton military reservation to a tract two miles wide and eight miles long, straddling the Rio Bonito lengthwise. The balance of the reservation, opened to settlement, was made subject to the public land laws.[42]

One year later, Congress established a reservation for the Mescaleros near Fort Stanton. This put the fort in a good position to watch over the Mescaleros and keep them on the reservation. Not everyone was satisfied with Congressional action regarding Fort Stanton and the Mescalero reservation, however. In January 1874, General Pope strongly urged the fort be closed and all New Mexico Apaches be concentrated at the Tularosa reservation. On November 20, 1871, Gen. Philip H. Sheridan, commander of the Division of the Missouri, had ordered the establishment of the Tularosa reservation. The Army located the reservation in the Tularosa Mountains close to the Arizona border, about 200 miles west of Fort Stanton, near present day Aragon. General Pope argued that moving the Mescaleros to the Tularosa reservation would greatly simplify the problems with the Apaches and save the Army a substantial amount of money. The Tularosa reservation closed in 1874, shortly after Pope's proposal, because of poor conditions there.[43] The Tularosa River, upon which the reservation was established, is distinct from the Rio Tularosa, which is located in the

A group of non-commissioned officers of the Third Infantry lounges on a porch. Note the adobe walls. This is probably the commissary storeroom or the sutler's store, because when the fort was built, only the hospital and commissary storerooms were made of adobe. *Courtesy Museum of New Mexico, Neg. No. 11668*

Companies E & I, 13th Infantry and H & D, 6th Cavalry on parade at Fort Stanton, 1885. The army adopted the plumed and spiked helmets in emulation of the German Army. Note the lack of grass on the parade ground; there was little water for such niceties as grass. *Courtesy Museum of New Mexico, Neg. No. 77640*

Sacramento Mountains and runs from the South Fork River to the present town of Tularosa.

Reduction of the Fort Stanton reserve in 1872 did not attract much attention. A few New Mexico papers mentioned the action in three- or four-line comments in the local gossip section or in columns titled "From the Telegraph." The newly opened land not only had an abundance of rich grasses and fertile farmland, it was believed to bear gold in substantial quantities in the mountains west of Lincoln. About the same time the military reserve was reduced, some Navajos offered to show Estanislaus Luna where he could find gold in the White Mountains, west of Fort Stanton, in return for half his herd of sheep. Luna, taking a hundred men with him, accompanied the Navajos in search of the gold. Prospectors found gold and silver in the Sierra Blancas, or White Mountains, within the decade. Fortunately, settlers failed to avail themselves of the new farmlands and mineral wealth. Almost two years later, when the Department of the Interior expanded the Mescalero reservation so that it completely surrounded the reduced Fort Stanton reserve, it was not necessary to move people out of the area.[44]

The establishment of a Mescalero reservation in May 1873 was the culmination of more than ten years of effort that had begun when General Carleton sent the Mescaleros to Bosque Redondo. Indian agents Lorenzo Labadi and Michael Steck argued strongly for a separate reservation for the Mescaleros in November of 1862.[45] In January 1866, Superintendent of Indian Affairs Felipe Delgado recommended a reservation for Jicarilla and Mescalero Apaches near Fort Stanton, and in 1867 Superintendent of Indian Affairs A. Baldwin Norton urged that a Mescalero reservation be established fifty miles southeast of Fort Stanton. Secretary of the Interior Orville H. Browning would not approve any of these plans unless Congress abandoned Bosque Redondo. In July 1867, Congressional Delegate J. Francisco Chavez proposed a plan to end Mescalero hostilities by settling them on a reservation in their homelands near the Rio Felix. This plan failed because negotiators were unable to make contact with the Mescaleros.[46]

Sentiment in favor of a reservation specifically for the Mescaleros was still strong when newly appointed Superintendent of Indian Affairs for New Mexico, Edwin L. Dudley, visited the Mescalero agency at Fort Stanton in December 1872. Dudley found that the post traders, L. G. Murphy & Co., had taken over agency affairs, overriding the authority of the Indian agent. They were defrauding the government while the Indians were starving. Dudley persuaded Secretary of the Interior Columbus Delano that a separate reservation for the Mescaleros was needed and in May, President Ulysses S. Grant approved the establishment of a Mescalero reservation bordering on the reduced Fort Stanton reserve. In February 1874, the Interior Department redefined the reservation so that it surrounded the military preserve, placing the fort in a dominant position over the Mescaleros. By 1880, prospectors had found gold and silver within the Mescalero reservation, west of Fort Stanton in the Sierra Blancas. In 1882, the Interior Department moved the Mescalero reservation to its present location, about eighteen miles from Fort Stanton and away from the valuable mineral deposits.[47]

While the Mescaleros were off the reservation and raiding the settlements, the Indian agency did little business and required few provisions. After Mescalero Indian agent Andrew J. Curtis established peace, the agency required provisions for its charges. Large numbers of

Indians came to the vicinity of the fort to live and draw rations at the agency, opening a substantial market for the local citizens. In 1872, even before a reservation was officially established, more than 750 Indians lived in the neighborhood of Fort Stanton and drew rations from the agency at the fort. Official establishment of the reservation effectively guaranteed this market for some time to come. The actual quantity of food and supplies furnished to the agency by the post trader, L. G. Murphy & Co., cannot be determined because of that company's fraudulent practices.[48]

In August 1872, L. G. Murphy & Co. charged the government $11,543 for feeding 1,895 Indians. Indian Agent Curtis later pointed out that only 760 people drew rations at the time. In March 1873, when newly-arrived agent Samuel B. Bushnell attempted to exercise his authority, Lawrence Murphy threatened to bring on an Indian uprising. Believing the post commander, Captain Chambers McKibbin, to be in league with Murphy, Bushnell warned McKibbin that he had learned, from citizens, of a possible Indian uprising. Bushnell later realized McKibbin was not in association with Murphy and told McKibbin what was happening. McKibbin immediately reported the whole affair to Headquarters, District of New Mexico. Later that year, one of Murphy's clerks fired a shot at one of the post officers during an argument with another man. Shortly after that the Army expelled L. G. Murphy & Co. from the post. Official records do not state any reason for the expulsion and the company retained its post tradership. The following year, General Pope complained to Secretary of War Belknap that L. G. Murphy & Co. was interfering in the operation of the Mescalero agency and the company controlled all crops in the area as well as the supplies for Fort Stanton and the Mescalero agency, keeping prices needlessly high.[49]

Much has been written about Lawrence G. Murphy's attempts to control the local economy and the subject is beyond the scope of this book. However, L. G. Murphy & Co. had the only post tradership in the region, making it the dominant economic institution in the area. The firm's operations affected the relationship between Fort Stanton and the community to the point that an attempt in 1878 to supplant L. G. Murphy & Co. as the economic power in the region, known as the Lincoln County War, involved the post garrison in a bloody civil disturbance. The company, which constituted the most substantial market for local farmers' and ranchers' produce, was central to nearly all business transactions in the community and was often accused of fraud and gouging. Although L. G. Murphy & Co. did defraud the government by inflating the number of Indians receiving rations at the agency, allegations that the firm charged exorbitant prices and monopolized business in the region are not supported by the evidence. Prices paid and prices charged by L. G. Murphy & Co. were in line with prices paid and charged throughout the territory.[50]

While L. G. Murphy & Co. delivered more hay to Fort Stanton than any other single supplier, they did not exercise a monopoly. Competition for contracts at military posts was keen and between 1865 and 1879 contracts to supply hay to Fort Stanton were awarded to fifteen different venders including Henry Lesinskey and Company of Las Cruces and Lehman Spielberg of Santa Fe. Both firms had a much larger financial base than L. G. Murphy & Co. In 1868 Henry Lesinskey and Company did as much business in one month as L. G. Murphy & Co. did the entire year. From 1867 through 1878, L. G. Murphy & Co. held only thirty-one percent of the Fort Stanton quartermaster and commissary contracts. During that time contracts also went to at least fifteen other venders, including Willi Spiegelberg and Benjamin Schuster of Santa Fe, Patrick Coghlan of Tularosa, Peter Ott of Doña Ana County, and local residents Jose Montaño, Paul Dowlin, Elisha Dow, and Frank Lesnett.[51]

Although L. G. Murphy & Co. was not the only purveyor delivering goods to Fort Stanton, it constituted the largest market in the Rio Bonito area. Jose Montaño, Isaac Ellis, and others had stores in Lincoln, but their market was limited. In 1871 a firm named Bliss & Lombard opened a post tradership at Fort Stanton also. Ltc. August V. Kautz noted that because of their positions as post traders, all the settlers in the region were compelled to come to these two stores for supplies. Murphy bought out Bliss & Lombard in 1872, leaving only one post trader in Lincoln. L. G. Murphy & Co. was not simply trading with the Army and selling provisions to the Mescalero agency. In Lincoln, the company operated the Samuel Wortley's Mess, a saloon supplied by its own brewery, and a billiard room. As the biggest and most diversified business in Lincoln, L. G. Murphy & Co.'s main problem was cash flow. However, contracts with the post and the Indian agency constituted virtually the only source of liquid, or cash, assets for the organization and the surrounding community. While the company did not monopolize business in the region, it did try to monopolize the cash in the region.[52]

L. G. Murphy & Co. operated in a nearly cashless environment. The only currency in the region was a dwindling supply of Mexican silver coins. The business community used Government vouchers and promissory notes, which were transferable, as cash. Barter was a common way of conducting trade and the settlers in the area obtained the seed, tools, and supplies needed to continue operations from L. G. Murphy & Co. in return for consignments of grain, beef, or other produce. Some of the more successful farmers and ranchers in the region, such as Jose Montaño, were able to do business independently with the fort or with other contractors, but the presence of L. G. Murphy & Co. was critical to the survival of most of the settlers in the area, who had nowhere else to sell or barter their produce or to obtain needed supplies. Similarly, Fort Stanton, and the Mescalero agency, were critical to L. G. Murphy & Co., which had few other practical markets. L. G. Murphy & Co. had other enterprises, but they did not bring in enough business to sustain the company. By the 1870s the importance of Fort Stanton in the economy of the region was declining, though it remained a significant factor.[53]

In 1870, Lincoln County, with less than two percent of New Mexico's population, produced twenty-one percent of the territory's corn. Agricultural produce purchased by Fort Stanton represented only six percent of the local production. In 1872, L. G. Murphy & Co. contracted to deliver 1.2 million pounds of corn to Forts Stanton and Tularosa. This represented only sixteen percent of the area's corn crop. Although the post probably bought local corn from other venders as well, this left a substantial amount to be sold elsewhere or lost. The population grew and the settlers continued to produce bountiful crops, even in times of drought and other disasters. In the last half of the decade, Government purchases, including those by the Mescalero agency, were considerably less than local production. By 1878 L. G. Murphy & Co. had folded and was taken over by James J. Dolan. This business also failed. Clearly, area farmers and ranchers had to find other markets for their goods or move on. Between 1870 and 1880, the population in the region increased by thirty-nine percent. The fact that the population grew, and the farmers continued to produce increasingly larger crops at a time when the post and Mescalero agency could absorb only a small fraction of their produce, demonstrates that area settlers were not as dependent upon Fort Stanton as General Pope and Secretary Belknap believed.[54]

Although Fort Stanton was declining in importance to the regional economy and ranking officers such as General Pope felt the post should be closed, it was still important to the region. Fort Stanton was the only governmental institution that could be relied upon for protection from rustlers and other criminal elements. The fort had the only jail around and constituted the only law enforcement force of any size.[55] However, the customary use of troops from Fort Stanton as *posse comitatus* eventually produced some undesirable results.

Notes to Chapter III

1. Hays, p. 55.

2. Brady to Chapman, June 27, Fritz to Cutler, June 23, Fritz to Taylor, July 26, and Brady to Commanding Officer, Fort Sumner, July 4, 1865, *Letters Received, Dept. of NM*, roll 26, B216, F32, F46 and B257; *Fort Stanton Returns*, roll 1216, post returns, May, June, July, 1865; Hays, pp. 55–56, 64, 65–67.

3. Brady to Chapman, June 27, 1865, *Letters Received, Dept. of NM*, roll 26, B216.

4. Ibid.

5. Fritz to Cutler, June 23, and Fritz to Taylor, July 26, 1865, *Letters Received, Dept. of NM*, roll 26, F32 and F46; Brady to Chapman, June 27, 1865, *Letters Received, Dept. of NM*, roll 26, B216; Brady to Cutler, Aug. 11, 1865, *Letters Received by Headquarters, District of New Mexico, September 1865 to August 1890*, RG 393, Microcopy M1088, (NARS) (Hereafter referred to as *Letters Received, Dist. of NM*), roll 1, B417.

6. Brady to Chapman, June 27, 1865, *Letters Received, Dept. of NM*, roll 26, B216.

7. *Fort Stanton Returns*, roll 1216, post returns, Jan. 1865–Feb. 1866; Brady to Commanding Officer, Fort Sumner, July 4, 1865, *Letters Received, Dept. of NM*, roll 26, B257; Brady to Cutler, Sept. 8, 1865, *Letters Received, Dist. of NM*, roll 1, B417.

8. Russell to DeForrest, Aug. 18, and Russell to DeForrest, Sept. 16, 1867, *Letters Received, Dist. of NM*, roll 8, S208, S253.

9. Miller, *Soldiers and Settlers*, pp. 219–20.

10. Miller, *Soldiers and Settlers*, pp. 220–21; *Fort Stanton Returns*, roll 1216, post return, Oct. 1864; Enos to McFerran, Oct. 24, 1864, *Letters Received, Dept. of NM*, roll 23, E154; Carleton to Commanding Officer, Fort Stanton, Oct. 26, and Carleton to Thomas, Nov. 7, 1864, *Letters Sent*, roll 3, vol. 11, #932, #945.

11. *Letters Received, Dist. of NM*, Introduction, p. 1; *Letters Received, Dept. of NM*, Introduction, p. 1.

12. Miller, *Soldiers and Settlers*, p. 220; Wilson, *Merchants, Guns and Money*, pp. 24, 29; *Fort Stanton Returns*, roll 1216, post returns, Oct. 1865–Aug. 1866.

13. Miller, *Soldiers and Settlers*, p. 220; *Fort Stanton Returns*, roll 1217, post returns, Feb.–June, 1869.

14. *Fort Stanton Returns*, roll 1217, post returns, Oct. 1868–July 1869; Miller, *Soldiers and Settlers*, pp. 220–21.

15. *Fort Stanton Returns*, roll 1217, post returns, March 1868–Feb. 1872; Miller, *Soldiers and Settlers*, p. 221.

16. *Fort Stanton Returns*, roll 1217, post returns, Mar. 1868–Nov. 1871; Miller, *Soldiers and Settlers*, p. 220; Seckler and Hosmer, p. 29.

17. *8th Census; Population Schedules of the Ninth Census of the United States, 1870*, Microcopy 593, roll 898 (NARS) (hereafter referred to as *9th Census*).

18. Ibid.; Seckler and Hosmer, pp. 1, 15; Wilson, *Merchants, Guns and Money*, pp. 4, 10, 23, 24; Beck and Haas, pp. 43–46.

19. *8th Census; 9th Census;* Seckler and Hosmer, p. 29.

20. Carleton to Thomas, Sept. 30, 1863, *Official Records*, series 1, vol. 15, pp. 576–77; *8th Census;* Carson to Cutler, Jan. 4, 1863, *Letters Received, Dept. of NM*, roll 18, C24; *9th Census; Fort*

Stanton Returns, roll 1217, post return, June, 1866; Murphy to DeForrest, June 10, 1866, *Letters Received, Dist. of NM,* roll 3, M95, enclosure; Wilson, *Merchants, Guns and Money,* pp. 6, 19–22.

21. For examples of the service men's and their wives' reactions to the beauty and abundance of the Hondo, Ruidoso and Bonito river valleys see Boyd, p. 164; Carson to Cutler, Jan. 4, 1863, *Letters Received, Dept. of NM,* roll 18, C24; Extracts from two private letters written by Bvt. Maj. James H. Carleton and published in the *Santa Fe Weekly Gazette,* Apr. 28, 1855, p. 2, quoted in Wilson, *Merchants, Guns and Money,* pp. 3–4; Miles to Garland, May 11, 1855, *Letters Received, Dept. of NM,* roll 4, M29.

22. *9th Census; Fort Stanton Returns,* roll 1216, post returns, Oct. 1865–Aug. 1866, roll 1217, post returns, Mar.–June 1870; *Old Lincoln County Pioneer Stories: Interviews from the WPA Writer's Project,* (Lincoln, NM: Lincoln County Historical Society Publications, 1994), pp. 13, 15.

23. A statistical comparison of the two populations' origins of birth in 1870 strongly supports the proposition that former soldiers from the fort, and their relatives, often settled in the region. Hispanos were excluded because no Hispanic troops were stationed at Fort Stanton in 1870. Further, 97% of the Hispanos living in Lincoln had been born in New Mexico and where they may have migrated from is unclear. The populations considered were distributed as shown in the following chart.

Origin of birth	Lincoln	Ft. Stanton
United States	54	68
Ireland	11	25
Germany	5	11
Great Britain	0	10
Western Europe	0	3
Elsewhere	1	2

The *United States* includes the 37 states of the Union in 1870, *Germany* includes Germany, Bavaria, Prussia, Frankfurt Am Main, Wortemburg, Saxony and Poland, *Great Britain* includes

England, Scotland, and Wales, *Western Europe* includes Denmark, France and Spain, and *Elsewhere* includes Canada and the West Indies. A simple linear regression yielded a Pearson Product-Moment Correlation Coefficient of 0.985, indicating a close correlation between the ethnic mixture of the fort and that of the town. A Chi Square test for dependence, using the same values and testing for a 95% level of confidence indicated a dependent relationship. In other words, there is a 95% certainty that a correspondence existed between the Anglo ethnic makeup of the garrison at Fort Stanton and the Anglo ethnic makeup of the citizenry of Lincoln. See *9th Census*.

24. Utley, *Frontier Regulars*, p. 180; Brady to Cutler, Aug. 11, Brady to Cutler, Sept. 8, 1865, *Letters Received, Dist. of NM*, roll 1, B419, B417; Reeve to Easton, June 18, 1855, *Letters Received, Dept. of NM*, roll 4, R6; Brady to Chapman, June 27, 1865, *Letters Received, Dept. of NM*, roll 26, B216; Rickey, p. 203.

25. Brady to Cutler, Sept. 8, 1865, *Letters Received, Dist. of NM* roll 1, B417; *Fort Stanton Returns*, roll 1216, post returns, July–Oct. 1865.

26. Hays, pp. 64–68; *Fort Stanton Returns*, roll 1217, post returns, Oct. 1865–May 1866.

27. *Fort Stanton Returns*, roll 1216, post returns, Aug.–Oct. 1866; Alfred B. Thomas and Averam B. Bender, *Apache Indians*, vol. XI, (New York: Garland Publishing Inc., 1974), p. 219.

28. Thomas and Bender, p. 226.

29. *Fort Stanton Returns*, roll 1216, post returns, Aug.–Oct. 1866; Russell to DeForrest, July 29, and Russell to DeForrest, Aug. 11, 1867, *Letters Received, Dist. of NM*, roll 1218, 187, S201; Hays, pp. 70–71; Thomas and Bender, p. 247.

30. Hays, p. 72; Cushing to Post Adjutant, Jan. 8, 1870, *Department of New Mexico, Letters Received*, RG 98, (NARS), file S1, microfilm copy at New Mexico State Archives and Records Center, Santa Fe (hereafter referred to as "Cushing Report").

31. "Cushing Report"; *Fort Stanton Returns*, roll 1217, post returns, Nov.–Dec. 1869; Andrew I. Wallace, "Duty in the District of New Mexico: A Military Memoir," *New Mexico Historical Review*, 50 (July 1975): 244–45.

32. "Cushing Report"; *Fort Stanton Returns,* roll 1217, post return, Dec. 1869; Wallace, p. 245.

33. "Cushing Report."

34. Ibid.

35. "Cushing Report"; "Report to AAAG regarding a Scout of December 19, 1869–January 6, 1870 from Fort Stanton, January 8, 1870", copy at the Lincoln County Heritage Trust Museum, Lincoln, New Mexico; *Fort Stanton Returns,* roll 1217, post returns, Dec. 1869–Feb. 1870; Kautz to AAAG, Feb. 8, 1870, *Letters Received, Dist. of NM,* roll 11, S19; Wallace, pp. 245–246.

36. Monahan to DeForrest, Feb. 4, 1867, *Letters Received, Dist. of NM,* roll 8, S61, enclosure; Hays, pp. 69–70.

37. McKibbin to AAAG, District of New Mexico, Nov. 3, 1870, *Letters Received, Dist. of NM,* roll 11, target 2, S159.
    Note: for examples of some of the scouts and fights see *Fort Stanton Returns,* roll 1217, post returns, July–Aug. 1869, Sept.–Nov. 1870.

38. Kautz to AAAG, District of New Mexico, May 26, 1870, *Letters Received, Dist. of NM,* roll 11, S80; Brooke to Kobbe, Sept. 14, 1868, *Letters Received, Dist. of NM,* roll 10, S330; Wallace, p. 249; Boyd, p. viii, 170; Taylor F. Ealy, *Missionaries, Outlaws, and Indians: Taylor F. Ealy at Lincoln and Zuni, 1878–1881,* Norman J. Bender, ed. (Albuquerque: University of New Mexico Press, 1984) p. 45.

39. Thomas and Bender, pp. 256–58, 259; *Fort Stanton Returns,* roll 1217, post returns, July–Sept. 1869, May 1871–May 1872.

40. Hays, p. 71; Campbell to Delano, May 19, 1871, *Records of the New Mexico Superintendency of Indian Affairs, 1849–80,* Microcopy T-21, (NARS) roll 7, Letters Received; Belknap to Secretary of Interior, Jan 27, 1874, enclosures, in Department of the Interior to War Department, Jan. 27, 1874, included in Brady Appointment Papers, *Interior Department Appointment Papers; Territory of New Mexico, 1850–1907,* RG 48, "Records of the Office of the Secretary of the Interior," Microcopy M750, 18 rolls, (NARS) (hereafter referred to as ID AP), roll 1; Thomas and Bender, pp. 243–44, 246; Wilson, *Merchants, Guns and Money,* p. 24.

41. McKibbin to Williams, Apr. 29, 1873, *Letters Received, Dist. of NM*, roll 20, S65.

42. The Santa Fe *Daily New Mexican*, May 22, 1873, p. 1; The Santa Fe *Weekly New Mexican*, May 28, 1873, p. 1; *The Borderer*, Las Cruces, May 29, 1873, p. 1; Thomas and Bender, pp. 264–65; Hays, p. 91; ID AP; Lincoln County Heritage Trust, "Chronological History of Fort Stanton," (Lincoln, NM: Lincoln County Heritage Trust, n.d.), p. 1.

43. Belknap to Secretary of Interior, Jan. 27, 1874, with enclosures, ID AP; Sheridan to Granger, Nov. 20, 1871, *Letters Received, Dist. of NM*, roll 18, M264; Giese, p. 19.

44. The Santa Fe *Daily New Mexican*, May 22, 1873, p. 1; The Santa Fe *Weekly New Mexican*, May 28, 1873, p. 1; *The Borderer*, Las Cruces, May 29, 1873, p. 1; Thomas and Bender, pp. 264–65, 272–73; Hays, pp. 143, 154.

45. Carleton to Thomas, Feb. 1, 1863, *Official Records*, series 1, vol. 15, pp. 669–70; Miller, "General James Henry Carleton," p. 62; Morrison to Cutler, Nov. 24, and Morrison to Cutler, Nov 22, 1862, *Letters Received, Dept. of NM*, roll 17, M273, M274; Thomas and Bender, pp. 183–85.

46. Thomas and Bender, pp. 103–04, 220, 243–44, 247, 245; *Fort Stanton Returns*, roll 1216, post returns, Aug.–Oct. 1866; Russell to DeForrest, July 29, and Russell to DeForrest, Aug. 11, 1867, *Letters Received, Dist. of NM*, roll 1218, S187, S201.

47. Lincoln County Heritage Trust, pp. 1–2; Bushnell to Price, Dec. 15, Price to Pope, Dec. 19, enclosures, and Murphy to Campbell, May 4, 1873, ID AP; Hays, pp. 89, 90–91, 143, 154; Wilson, *Merchants, Guns and Money*, pp. 34–35, 130; Thomas and Bender, pp. 272–73.

48. Thomas and Bender, pp. 257–58; Wilson, *Merchants, Guns and Money*, pp. 34–35; McKibbin to AAAG, May 15, 1873, *Letters Received, Dist. of NM*, roll 20, S62, with enclosures.

49. Bushnell to McKibbin, May 14, and McKibbin to AAAG, May 15, 1873, *Letters Received, Dist. of NM*, roll 20, S75, S62, with enclosures; Bushnell to Price, Dec. 15, Price to Pope, Dec. 19, 1873, and Belknap to Secretary of Interior, Jan. 27, 1874, with enclosures, ID AP; Wilson, *Merchants, Guns and Money*, pp. 6, 30, 34–35, 130, 137.

50. Belknap to Secretary of Interior, Jan. 27, 1874, with enclosures, ID AP; Wilson, *Merchants, Guns and Money,* pp. 34–35, 41.

51. Wilson, *Merchants, Guns and Money,* pp. 40, 41, 29–34, 37; Miller, *Soldiers and Settlers,* pp. 61, 103–04, 343, 344–45.

52. Ibid.

53. Miller, *Soldiers and Settlers,* p. 61–62, 102, 344, 400 note 106; Wilson, *Merchants, Guns and Money,* pp. 27–43, 75–76.

54. Ibid.; Miller, *Soldiers and Settlers,* pp. 63–64; *9th Census; Population Schedules of the Tenth Census of the United States, 1880,* Microcopy T-9, roll 802, (NARS) (hereafter referred to as *10th Census*).

55. Wilson, *Merchants, Guns and Money,* p. 50.

Chapter IV

CIVIL STRIFE

As the Indian troubles subsided and the debate over closing Fort Stanton continued, law enforcement and civil matters played a more prominent roll in the activities of the garrison at Fort Stanton. This was especially true with regard to the communities of Tularosa and Lincoln. As communications and transportation improved and the post became more involved in municipal concerns, the mutually beneficial relationship between fort and community declined. The relationship became intrusive in the 1870s when Fort Stanton troops interfered in conflicts between civilians, directly affecting the course of events in at least one instance. By 1880 the post could absorb only a small portion of what the community produced and the community was forced to find other markets. During the 1880s, Indian problems essentially ended and the importance of the post, both militarily and economically, diminished substantially.[1]

In the late 1860s, thieves and rustlers created a genuine need for military assistance. Fort Stanton was the one government institution that could be relied upon for protection. It had the only law enforcement force of any size in the region, and the only jail. The guardhouse at Fort Stanton continually housed criminals awaiting action by the civilian courts. In June 1867, pickets arrested Mr. Frank Richards, with two stolen horses, and sent him to Fort Stanton in irons. Lt. Gerald G. Russell, commanding the post, asked Headquarters if he could transfer Richards because he did not have enough men to guard the prisoner and perform all the duties required of the garrison. Headquarters found no other secure lockup available to house the prisoner, and he remained at Fort Stanton. By 1868, the probate Judge in Lincoln customarily incarcerated his prisoners in the guardhouse at the fort. In December 1869, soldiers from Fort Stanton caught two civilians, John O. Tolliver and William Oswald, trying to steal some mules. The county probate judge directed that they be incarcerated in the post jail to await trial by civil authority. There is a notation regarding prisoners placed in the guardhouse at the direction of the Probate Judge of Lincoln County in almost every Fort Stanton post return from 1869 through 1872.[2]

In 1873, a conflict over water in the Tularosa Valley began a series of incidents that increasingly involved the garrison at Fort Stanton in civil affairs. The town of Tularosa was first settled in 1861 after floods and poor crops forced the people of a small Hispanic community named Colorado, on the Rio Grande north of Las Cruces, to relocate. They settled in the Tularosa Valley at the present town site. This agricultural community depended heavily on the waters of the Rio Tularosa. Following the Civil War some discharged veterans of the California Column settled in Tularosa Canyon, upstream from the village. The new settlers used the water from the river to irrigate their crops. This situation led to conflict between the Anglos in the canyon and the Hispanos in the town.[3] In September 1871, Col. August V. Kautz, commanding Fort Stanton, anticipated serious trouble during elections in Tularosa, 53 miles to the southeast, and sent a detail to the village on September 2 to quell any disturbances that might occur. No problems arose and five days later the detail returned to the post.[4] This was not the last time troops from Fort Stanton came to Tularosa. However, soldiers from the post had to quell a race war in Lincoln first.

In February 1873, three Anglo men from the Coe ranch near Lincoln, belonging to George Coe, pursued thieves who had stolen horses and other property from the ranch. They caught two of the men, Hispanos, with some of the stolen property. The posse killed both men, one when he resisted arrest and the other when he tried to escape. At Fort Stanton the post commander told them to report the incident to the probate judge. The judge said he had no authority in the matter but the county clerk, Juan B. Patron, tried to arrest them. Fearing for their lives at the hands of Hispanos, the posse members fled. The next day, County Commissioner William Brady requested troops from the fort to help control a crowd of Hispanos that was threatening life and property at the Coe ranch. Taking fifteen, men Captain McKibbin accompanied Brady to the ranch where they arrested twelve Hispanos. Here McKibbin demonstrated his own prejudice, and a propensity to threaten civil authorities, when he threatened to hold Patron hostage for the safety of the Anglos if any more trouble occurred.[5]

Civilian affairs within the reach of Fort Stanton's influence remained calm until May, when the conflict over water in Tularosa erupted into violence. Andrew J. Wilson and other Anglo farmers in Tularosa Canyon dammed the river, cutting off water from everyone downstream. The constable of Tularosa sent a group of townspeople to restore the flow of water in the river. The posse, led by Jose Marcos and Felipe Bernal, destroyed the dams. When Wilson and the others tried to rebuild the dams, they were fired upon by the Tularosans. Wilson and his neighbors petitioned Captain McKibbin for protection. McKibbin, who had already displayed a bias against Hispanics, made no effort to seek an equitable settlement but directly interfered in the matter, using his troops to impose his will upon United States citizens.[6]

McKibbin told the *alcalde* of Tularosa that he would be held personally responsible for any further violence on the part of the citizens of Tularosa and dispatched 2nd Lt. John W. Wilkinson, with five men, to the site of the trouble to protect the farmers while they rebuilt the dams. While attempts to prevent reconstruction of the dams were being turned away by Wilkinson's men, an armed posse of citizens arrived from Tularosa. A gunfight ensued in which one of the Tularosans was killed. Wilkinson sent a courier to the fort for help while the soldiers and farmers retreated to Blazer's Mill, thirty miles south of the post on the Ruidoso River. The villagers besieged the party at Blazer's Mill until Captain McKibbin arrived with more troops and a field piece.[7]

After dispersing the crowd at Blazer's Mill, McKibbin proceeded to Tularosa with the cannon. When the parish priest, Father Peter Lassaigne, pointed out that McKibbin had no authority there, McKibbin threatened to enter the town by force and to hang the priest if his troops were fired upon. The people of the town, intimidated by the gun, acquiesced and the troops spent the night in Tularosa without incident.

St. Francis de Paulo Church in Tularosa as it appears today. Father Lassaigne, who challenged Captain McKibbin's authority to use troops to occupy Tularosa, was pastor of this church. *Courtesy of the author*

McKibbin later claimed that he believed fear of personal harm was the only thing that would keep the priest from inciting more trouble.[8]

The Grand Jury of Doña Ana County met in June and indicted McKibbin for "unwarranted and tyrannical conduct," stating that he had no authority in the situation. The indictment pointed out that McKibbin had taken action in contravention of legally constituted authority, specifically the constable of Tularosa. The Army took no disciplinary action against McKibbin but General Order number three, from the Adjutant General's Office, was promulgated on February 14, 1874. This order prohibited the use of troops to enforce the laws of a state or territory and may have been influenced in part by Captain McKibbin's actions. This incident, known as the Tularosa Ditch War, did not end the trouble over water rights in the Tularosa Valley, which continued into the twentieth century, but it demonstrated one of the pitfalls of involving troops in citizens' quarrels.[9]

While the Tularosa Ditch War was in progress, the five Horrell brothers from Texas, wanted by Texas authorities, settled near Lincoln. Before the year ended the Horrells were involved in several shootings and anarchy reigned in the community. Fort Stanton was called upon to restore peace. Officers at the post apparently had learned from the Tularosa Ditch War, and troops from the fort did not get directly involved in the conflict. However, through timely displays of military presence, they ended the conflict with a minimum of bloodshed. Trouble started in December when Ben Horrell went into Lincoln with former Lincoln County sheriff Jack Gylam and three other men. In a house of prostitution the men, intoxicated, began firing their pistols and threatening other guests. When the town constable, Juan Martinez, arrived with five deputies, one of the Texans, David Warner, shot and killed Martinez. Warner and two others were killed in the gunfight that ensued. Horrell and Gylam fled but were caught and killed. Ben's brothers came to Lincoln seeking justice for the murders of their brother and Gylam. They received no satisfaction and left town threatening to retaliate.[10]

Three days later two prominent Hispano citizens of Lincoln were found murdered at the Horrell ranch and Hispanos from the town attempted to burn the Horrells out. In response, the Horrells went into Lincoln on December 20 and fired shots indiscriminately into the guests at a wedding celebration, killing four and wounding several more. Having lost control of the situation, the probate judge and justice of the peace resigned and fled. The townspeople petitioned the fort for protection and New Mexico Governor Marsh Giddings ordered the post commander, Maj. John L. Mason, to send troops into Lincoln to restore order. Mason sent troops on December 24 with orders to camp a half mile from town but not interfere. The soldiers' presence prevented a full-scale riot, but the Horrells were still at large and Giddings petitioned Col. John I. Grigg, commanding the District of New Mexico, for military assistance. When Grigg refused, Secretary of the Interior Columbus Delano asked Secretary of War William W. Belknap to authorize the use of troops in Lincoln. Belknap refused, stating that military force could only be used by a U.S. Marshall to carry out the orders of U.S. courts.[11]

Before the end of December, armed groups of men wandered around shooting at each other. Early in January 1874, Judge Warren Bristol, in Santa Fe, issued warrants for the arrest of the Horrells. Maj. William R. Price, who was leaving for Fort Stanton, agreed to hold the warrants until the court met.[12] Finally, on January 20, Sheriff

Officers in front of officers' quarters, Christmas 1871–72. *left to right:* Dr. Charles Styer, Lt. Orsemus Boyd (seated), Emil Fritz, Capt. Chambers McKibbin, Ltc. August Kautz (seated), Capt. William McCleave, Mrs. McKibbin or Boyd (seated), Lt. Casper H. Conrad, Mrs. Boyd or McKibbin (seated), and Lawrence G. Murphy. *Courtesy Museum of New Mexico, Neg. No. 101417*

Alexander H. Mills took a posse to the Horrell ranch to arrest the Horrells. They would not surrender and exchanged shots with the posse. Major Mason sent Captain McKibbin and his company to camp near the Horrell ranch, with instructions not to interfere. That night the Horrells quietly snuck away and the posse returned to Lincoln. Before leaving, the Horrells accepted promissory notes from James J. Dolan for their cattle. The Horrells did not know that Dolan represented L. G. Murphy & Co., whom they distrusted. On January 24, a few days after the Horrells left, Dolan raised another posse and returned to the Horrell ranch. The posse looted the ranch and burned it, returning to Lincoln with 600 bushels of wheat. The arrival of troops ended the affair without further bloodshed.[13]

Even though Fort Stanton remained "uninvolved," the troops did exert influence in the affair and soldiers from the post quieted matters on two occasions. On December 24, soldiers from the fort camped near Lincoln, intimidating unruly crowds and defusing a riotous situation, and on January 20, the Horrells simply abandoned the fight and fled when troops camped near their ranch. In both cases the parties involved were unaware that the soldiers would not take any action; their simple presence restored order. In March, a special election made Lawrence G. Murphy probate judge and Jose Piño y Piño justice of the peace. By April, an uneasy quiet had returned to the area. The town of Lincoln held a big Saint Patrick's Day celebration in which a large part of the Hispanic community participated. Nonetheless, the Tularosa Ditch War and the Horrell War left the area bitterly divided along ethnic lines.[14]

Four years after the Horrell War, the Lincoln County War again brought civil strife to the region. This time attempts to "show the flag," which had been effective in the Horrell War, were mismanaged by a commander who was predisposed in favor of one of the factions. As a result, troops from Fort Stanton interfered directly in civilian concerns, determining the outcome. This affair brought about the removal of the governor of New Mexico.[15]

The Lincoln County War was essentially a struggle between two groups of entrepreneurs who sought to gain economic dominance of the region: L. G. Murphy & Co. and Alexander McSween and his associates. In 1876–77 L. G. Murphy & Co., known as the House, was the economic and political power in the region. McSween, a young lawyer from Canada, allied himself in 1876 with John S. Chisum, a Texas cattle baron who had started ranching on the Pecos River. The presence of a large-scale rancher and farmer in the region

Staff of L.G. Murphy & Co., c 1868–77. *left to right*: James J. Dolan, Emil Fritz, William J. Martin, and Lawrence G. Murphy. *Courtesy Museum of New Mexico, Neg. No. 104912*

Post trader's store, c. 1886–90. L.G. Murphy & Co. sold the building to the Army. John Delaney occupied the building as post trader in 1881.
Courtesy Museum of New Mexico, Neg. No. 11656

threatened the economic dominance of the House. To aggravate the situation, John H. Tunstall, a young Englishman with money to invest, arrived in Lincoln in 1877 and promptly allied himself with McSween and Chisum, announcing his intentions to supplant the House as the economic force in the region. The irritant that ignited the violent phase of the Lincoln County War was a $10,000 life insurance policy that Emil Fritz had taken out before his death in 1874. The House claimed to be the beneficiary but, as executor of the estate, McSween asserted that the money belonged to Fritz's heirs and refused payment.[16]

In February 1878, Murphy accused McSween of embezzlement and district Judge Warren Bristol issued writs of attachment on McSween's holdings. Sheriff William Brady attached Tunstall's property as well, sending a deputy to Tunstall's ranch with a posse to attach the cattle. Tunstall was not at his ranch but the posse encountered him on their return trip and killed him. Emotions over the killing ran high and, fearing serious civil strife, Governor Samuel B. Axtell requested military assistance from President Rutherford B. Hays. Hays granted the request and the post commander at Fort Stanton, Capt. George Purington, received orders to support the "proper authorities." But both sides had law officers and judges issuing warrants. Purington decided to simply protect women and children and, leaving eight men in Lincoln as observers, requested further instructions from Headquarters. General Pope instructed Col. Edward Hatch, the newly arrived commander of the District of New Mexico, not to place troops at the disposal of the sheriff.[17]

In March the violence escalated when a posse of McSween men, calling themselves "Regulators" and armed with a warrant issued by Justice of the Peace John B. Wilson, killed three men. Two of these

John H. Tunstall
Courtesy Museum of New Mexico, Neg. No. 89683

men were members of the posse that had killed Tunstall, the third was a man whom they found to be a spy amongst them. On April 1, assailants, believed to be William Bonney and another man, shot and killed Sheriff Brady and a deputy in town. On April 5, two more men died in an affray at Blazer's Mill. On April 10, and again on April 20, Judge Bristol requested troops to guard the District Court while it was in session in Lincoln. Col. Nathan A. M. Dudley, who had just taken command at Fort Stanton, housed the judge at the fort and provided him with an escort.[18]

On June 25, Colonel Hatch received instructions that no further assistance by the troops of Fort Stanton was to be given to civil authorities in Lincoln County. Hatch advised Dudley of the directive, stipulating that troops no longer serve as *posse comitatus,* and specifically order-

William Brady
Courtesy Museum of New Mexico, Neg. No. 105103

ing Dudley not to use his troops in this way. By the time Dudley received these orders, he had sent Capt. Henry Carroll, with 36 men, in the company of Sheriff George W. Peppin, who replaced Brady, to the Coe Ranch to make arrests. Dudley promptly sent instructions to Captain Carroll to return to the post. Carroll immediately complied with the new orders, leaving Peppin to his own devices. In his reply to Hatch's orders, Dudley made it clear that he understood the Army's policy and that he was not to involve his troops in civilian affairs.[19]

With the army no longer involved, McSween decided to openly engage the House faction. On the evening of July 14, between forty and sixty men siding with McSween entered Lincoln after dark and took positions in McSween's house and nearby buildings. The following morning, more than fifty men of the House group took positions in Lincoln facing McSween's forces.[20] Sheriff Peppin sent a messenger to Fort Stanton requesting the loan of a howitzer. In his reply to Peppin, Dudley stated that he could not lend Peppin the gun, but expressed complete sympathy with the House side.[21] The messenger carrying Dudley's reply was nearly struck by bullets, probably coming from some of McSween's men. In the dispatch ordering Dudley not to use troops to assist civil authorities, Hatch had instructed Dudley to send

104

weekly reports to Headquarters regarding the situation in Lincoln. He did so, writing lengthy letters with numerous inclusions and exhibits each time. In his July 18 report, Dudley hinted at what he was about to do. Alluding to orders not to interfere, Dudley stated that his duty required that something be done to end the state of affairs in Lincoln. Dudley sent a group of officers with his messenger into Lincoln to investigate the incident. When these officers tried to aid a wounded man, the McSween forces continued to fire at him, narrowly missing the post surgeon. Dudley mounted every

Nathan Augustus Monroe Dudley
*Courtesy Museum of New Mexico,
Neg. No. 92936*

available man at the post and headed for Lincoln. He brought a howitzer, a Gatling Gun, three day's provisions, and enough ammunition to fight a major battle.[22]

Dudley's column marched into Lincoln on July 19 and established a camp south of the center of town between the opposing forces. Pointing the howitzer at the McSween house, Dudley threatened to use the gun if fired upon and issued an invitation for women, children, and noncombatants to come to his camp for protection. He then summoned Justice of the Peace John B. Wilson and ordered him to issue warrants for the arrest of McSween and others in the McSween faction. When Wilson demurred, Dudley threatened him. Thoroughly intimidated, Wilson complied. Against explicit orders to the contrary, Dudley then used his troops to assist Peppin in serving the warrants.[23]

Suzan McSween
Courtesy Center for Southwest Research,
General Library, University of New Mexico,
Neg. No. 000-021-0031

In the evening of July 19, Peppin asked the McSween men to surrender. When they refused, Peppin ordered the McSween house set afire. When McSween's wife pleaded with Dudley to stop the burning of her house, he refused. Under cover of darkness most of the McSween supporters escaped from the rear of the house but the Peppin posse killed McSween and three others as they tried to escape. Among those killed in the McSween house were five Hispanic men, including Francisco Zamora and Vicente Romero. Ygenio Salazar, who was badly wounded, crawled into the yard and played dead until the Peppin posse left. The next day, Peppin's posse got drunk and looted the Tunstall store. The townspeople soon joined in the looting while Dudley, ignoring the riot, returned to Fort Stanton. The day following the burning of the McSween house, relatives found a disoriented Ygenio Salazar wandering in town.[24]

At the start of the troubles in Lincoln, Captain Purington realized what was happening and was determined to keep his troops out of a no-win situation. But the new post commander, Colonel Dudley, felt frustrated by the Army's noninvolvement policy because by early May, he had already chosen sides. Dudley believed the McSween people were "lawless foreigners," and that the House men were honorable citizens trying to do their civic duty. Dudley told Colonel Hatch: "There are certain parties here who will have to be brought to justice or leave the Country [sic]." He indicated his strong inclination to become involved when he said, "Nothing but the strong arm of the military in my judgment will put a stop to the constant shedding of blood." Dudley admitted that Peppin had disreputable men in his posse, but excused this with the remark that Peppin's personal safety required them.[25] A contentious individual, prone to disobey orders when he disagreed with them,[26] Dudley found the first good excuse to interfere, which was bullets narrowly missing his men, and brought his troops into Lincoln. One cannot truly

Suzan McSween in her later years
Courtesy Center for Southwest Research,
General Library, University of New Mexico,
Neg. No. 000-021-0032

determine what the outcome might have been had Dudley not interfered, but it is clear that his interference contributed to the destruction of property and loss of life. However, as one newspaper editor wrote, the real fault lay with poor territorial administration and ineffective law enforcement at the outset. Dudley pointed out in May that ineffective law enforcement, and the seeming lack of involvement of territorial administrators, had allowed the situation to develop to a point where drastic action was required. He complained of known criminals walking the streets with no attempts to apprehend them, and of the district court making no effort to restore order.[27] A subsequent investigation of the affair by the United States Justice Department bears this out.

In August, the United States Department of Justice conducted an investigation into the events in Lincoln over the previous year. In September, General Lewis "Lew" Wallace replaced Governor Axtell as territorial governor. Lawlessness reigned supreme in Lincoln County as a result of the Lincoln County War and in October President Hays issued a proclamation permitting Wallace to use troops to regain control. Following a court-martial from which he emerged unscathed, Dudley took command of Fort Cummings. It took a long time for matters to settle in Lincoln County. In February 1879, Dolan partisans murdered the lawyer hired by Suzan McSween to settle her husband's affairs. But by 1880 peace had essentially been restored.[28]

In spite of the civil strife during the 1870s, the population in the region continued to grow. By 1880 the number of people living in Lincoln had risen to 638 and the configuration of the population had changed. In 1870 the ethnic makeup of the Anglo citizens of Lincoln closely resembled that of the residents of Fort Stanton. In 1880 this was no longer true. Of the 118 people living at Fort Stanton, including soldiers, women, children, servants, and civilian employees, Ninety came from the United States, five from Ireland, five from Germany, one from Switzerland, one from England, one from China, one from Brazil, and fourteen from New Mexico. Nine of the New Mexicans were children of soldiers, three were servants, and two were civilian employees.[29] The Anglo population of Lincoln included thirty-eight people born in New Mexico, thirty-one born within the thirty-eight states, one born in England, and two born in Mexico. For the first time, the number of Anglo residents born in New Mexico exceeded the number born elsewhere. The Hispanic citizens of Lincoln included 545 born in New Mexico and twenty-one born in Mexico. The percentage of the Hispanic residents born in New Mexico had increased from sixty-nine percent in 1870 to eighty-nine percent in 1880.[30]

Peaceful settlers were not the only people who came to Lincoln County during the 1870s. The civil strife and lack of effective law enforcement attracted the lawless. Mail carriers refused to carry the mail without an escort because robbers ran rampant, sometimes in bands as large as sixty. Rustlers targeted herds belonging to the Indians of the Mescalero reservation, causing much resentment. In June 1879, Agent Samuel A. Russell persuaded Victorio to come with his band to the Mescalero reservation. In August, after officials of Grant County indicted Victorio for murder, he left the Mescalero reservation with a gathering of Warm Springs and Mescalero Apaches, inaugurating the "Victorio War." Troops from Fort Stanton took part in the pursuit, which ended in the Tres Castillos Mountains of Mexico where Mexican troops killed Victorio in 1880. Chief Nana evaded the Mexicans and went on a two-month vengeance raid. A short time later, Apache chiefs Geronimo and Mangus left the San Carlos reservation in Arizona and kept the pursuing troops busy until the fall of 1886. Rebellious Indian leaders used the Mescalero reservation as a secret base and supply depot and, because of its proximity to both the Mexican border and the Mescalero Reservation, Fort Stanton played an important roll in the campaigns of 1879–86.[31] During this period the fort remained an important customer for the local farmers and ranchers.

The region's farms and ranches changed considerably between 1865 and 1880. During the years 1873–79, many farmers and ranchers, powerless against rustlers and unable to get help from the law, left the area. By 1880 the active farmland was in the hands of approximately twelve farmers. Three individuals owned roughly half of this land. Sales to the military remained important. Larger producers, such as Jose Montaño and Francisco Valencia, contracted with Fort Stanton and other consumers directly while the small farmers, lacking volume, sold their goods to contractors, primarily L. G. Murphy & Co. and its successors. The amount of land under cultivation had increased from 1,695 acres in 1870 to 2,111 acres in 1880. In 1879 the farms around Lincoln produced 21,000 bushels of corn, down from 23,000 in 1869. Yet Fort Stanton purchased only 2,679 bushels, or less than 13% of the crop. Although this was still a substantial market, the community could no longer depend solely on the fort as a market for its produce, except for hay. Fort Stanton had constant problems acquiring hay.[32]

In the 1870s hay was not raised, but cut from the grasses growing naturally in the area. As people founded new settlements and established farms, plowing the land that had formerly been hay fields, the hay supply decreased. Droughts, insects, and pests such as prairie dogs exacerbated the problems of supplying hay to the fort. A shortage of hay occurred in ten of the fifteen years from 1865 through 1879. A number of contractors were forced to travel so far to find hay that they lost money on their contracts. In 1871, Peter Ott, unable to locate hay to fulfill his contract, defaulted. Farmers or contractors sometimes syndicated to raise the price of hay. In 1870, more than 200 tons of hay at Fort Stanton was set afire by Indians and destroyed. Lawrence Murphy came to the rescue in a manner inconsistent with the image painted by his detractors. Having the only supply of hay in the area, he supplied hay to the post at the regular contract price when he could have charged considerably more. By 1879, railroad service had come to New Mexico, prompting the Chief Quartermaster, James Dana, to inquire into the cost of importing hay from Kansas.[33]

In April 1879, railroad service opened to Las Vegas and within a year freight shipments began arriving in Albuquerque. The railroad reduced the cost of transportation considerably and provided a more reliable supply of hay. By 1885 bailed hay from Kansas was cheaper than locally produced hay and some people argued that it was better. The railroad made the importation of other crops practical as well and products from New Mexico had to compete with lower priced products from outside the territory. The traditional crops of wheat and corn became a glut on the market and local farmers began raising fruit as an alternative. Local farmers also raised alfalfa to compete with the Kansas hay. However, even though the locally grown alfalfa was competitive in price with imported hay and local farmers supplied hay to half the posts in Arizona, the posts in New Mexico persisted in buying Kansas hay with only two exceptions. Forts Union and Stanton continued to purchase locally produced hay until they closed.[34]

The railroad was only one of the advancements in communication that reached Fort Stanton in the 1880s. On May 22, 1881, orders from District Headquarters directed that troops construct a telegraph line from Fort Stanton to "a point on the *Jornada* [*del Muerto*]," most likely to join with the line running from Mesilla to Santa Fe. Lt. Charles E. Gorst, two noncommissioned officers and eighteen privates left Fort Stanton on June 14 to construct the line, which they completed in September. Fort Stanton's telegraph, like the Army's roads and mail service before it, also served the civilian community. Mining in the region gradually developed and gold was discovered west of Lincoln. Miners in the area sometimes used the telegraph at the fort. In the fall of 1885, a telephone line between the fort and the Mescalero Agency went into operation, but Lincoln did not acquire its first telephone until after 1900.[35]

By 1886, the railroad telegraph and telephone had come to Fort Stanton and, with the surrender of Geronimo, the Indians were at peace. After 1886 life at Fort Stanton became routine. Although the fort no longer filled any important military need, it was still important to the community. The median monthly civilian payroll at Fort Stanton from April 1880 through December 1887, was about $800. It ranged from as high as $1,722 in February 1883 to as low as $390 in December 1884. In addition, the post still consumed about six percent of the locally produced grain. But in 1895 its economic contribution to the community did not justify keeping the fort open and General Order Number 56 directed that Fort Stanton be closed and the land turned over to the Department of the Interior. In January 1896, A Company, 1st Cavalry, the direct descendant of the 1st Dragoons that established the fort forty-one years earlier, departed the post. Company A was the last full military unit to occupy Fort Stanton. A caretaker detail remained at the fort to guard and ship all portable public property to other posts. Lt. William Black submitted the July post return, Fort Stanton's last. On August 17, Lieutenant Black reported, "I have the honor to report that the detachments at this post are withdrawn today and therefore no further returns will be submitted."[36]

Fort Stanton was not demolished. On April 1, 1899, President William McKinley set Fort Stanton aside for use as a tuberculosis hospital for the Merchant Marine. The Fort Stanton Marine Hospital was the first federal hospital exclusively for the treatment of tuberculosis, and was operated under the jurisdiction of the United States Public Health Service. This new facility had thirty-eight buildings and could accommodate 200 patients with quarters for the staff. The hospital admitted its first patient on November 1, 1899.[37]

Notes to Chapter IV

1. P. J. Rasch, "The Tularosa Ditch War", *New Mexico Historical Review*, 43 (July 1968): 229–35; Dee Dwight Greenly, "The Military Career of Nathan Augustus Monroe Dudley, 1843–1889," (Master's thesis, New Mexico State University, 1986), pp. 80–93.

2. Wilson, *Merchants, Guns and Money*, p. 50; Russell to DeForrest, June 29, 1867, *Letters Received, Dist. of NM*, roll 8, S163; Kautz to AAAG, District of New Mexico, Jan. 15, 1870, *Letters Received, Dist. of NM*, roll 11, S7; *Fort Stanton Returns*, roll 1217, post returns, Jan.–Mar. 1870.

3. Seckler and Hosmer, pp. 61, 63; Darlis A. Miller, *The California Column in New Mexico*, (Albuquerque: University of New Mexico Press, 1982), p. 107.

4. Hays, p. 90; *Fort Stanton Returns*, roll 1217, post return, Sept. 1871.

5. McKibbin to AAAG, Feb. 6, 1873, *Letters Received, Dist. of NM*, roll 20, S3, with enclosure; Billy Charles Patrick Cummings, *Frontier Parish*, (Lincoln, NM: Lincoln County Historical Society Publications, 1995), p. 22.

6. McKibbin to AAAG, Feb. 6, and McKibbin to AAAG, June 13, 1873, *Letters Received, Dist. of NM*, roll 20, S3 with enclosure, S36 with enclosures; Cummings, pp. 20, 21; Hays, pp. 90–91.

7. McKibbin to AAAG, June 13, 1873, *Letters Received, Dist. of NM*, roll 20, S36 with enclosures; Cummings, pp. 20, 21; Hays, pp. 90–91; Bond to Commanding Officer, District of New Mexico, July 2, 1873, *Letters Received, Dist. of NM*, roll 17, B11.

8. Ibid.; Wilson, *Merchants, Guns and Money*, p. 43.

9. McKibbin to AAAG, June 13, 1873, *Letters Received, Dist. of NM*, roll 20, S36, with enclosures; Bond to Commanding Officer, District of New Mexico, July 2, 1873, *Letters Received, Dist. of NM*, roll 17, B11; Rasch, pp. 230–31; Hays, p. 91; Wilson, *Merchants, Guns and Money*, p. 43.
Note: McKibbin's letter includes the Grand Jury's report and

Judge Warren Bristol's opinion. Bond's letter includes the Grand Jury's report.

10. The Santa Fe *Weekly New Mexican*, Dec. 16, 1873, p. 1; *Old Lincoln County Pioneer Stories*, p. 7; Wilson, *Merchants, Guns and Money*, p. 43; Hays, p. 107–08.

11. Mason to AAG, Dec. 25, 1873, *Letters Received, Dist. of NM*, roll 20, S121; Giddings to Grigg, Jan. 12, Giddings to Grigg, Feb. 5, 1874 *Letters Received, Dist. of NM*, roll 21, G2, G5; Price to AAAG, Jan. 18, 1874, *Letters Received, Dist. of NM*, roll 23, P2; The Santa Fe *Weekly New Mexican*, Feb. 10, 1874, p. 2; Cummings, p. 22; Wilson, *Merchants, Guns and Money*, pp. 44–46; Seckler and Hosmer, p. 4; Hays, p. 108.

12. Giddings to Grigg, Jan 12, 1874, *Letters Received, Dist. of NM*, roll 21, G2; Price to AAAG, Jan. 18, 1874, *Letters Received, Dist. of NM*, roll 23, P2, with enclosures; Wilson, *Merchants, Guns and Money*, pp. 44–47.

13. Price to AAAG, Jan. 26, Price to AAAG, Jan. 28, 1874, *Letters Received, Dist. of NM*, roll 23, P4, P5; The Santa Fe *Weekly New Mexican*, Feb. 3, 1874, p. 1, Feb. 10, 1874, p. 1; Wilson, *Merchants, Guns and Money*, pp. 46–48; Seckler and Hosmer, p. 4; Hays, p. 108.

14. Price to AAAG, Jan. 26, 1874, *Letters Received, Dist. of NM*, roll 23, P4; *Mesilla News*, April 11, 1874, p. 6; Wilson, *Merchants, Guns and Money*, p. 47.

15. *Mesilla Valley Independent*, Aug. 31, 1878, p. 2, Sept. 14, 1878, p. 2; William H. Leckie, *The Buffalo Soldiers: A Narrative of the Negro Cavalry in the West* (Norman: University of Oklahoma Press, 1985), p. 203.

16. *Mesilla Valley Independent*, Aug. 31, 1878, p. 2, Sept. 14, 1878, p. 2; McSween to Fritz, Dec. 14, 1876, and Gonzales to Donnell, Lawson and Company, Aug. 1, 1877, on display in the Old Lincoln County Courthouse, Lincoln State Monument, Lincoln, New Mexico; Wilson, *Merchants, Guns and Money*, pp. 27–29, 34–38, 40, 41, 58, 63, 67, 71; Leckie, pp. 193–94; Miller, *Soldiers and Settlers*, p. 343; Greenly, pp. 80–81, 90–93; Ealy, pp. 17, 28.

17. *Fort Stanton Returns,* roll 1218, post return, Feb. 1878; Ealy, pp. 17, 27–28; *Mesilla News,* July 6, 1878, p. 2; Wilson, *Merchants, Guns and Money,* pp. 58, 63, 79; Leckie, pp. 194–95.

18. *Mesilla News,* June 29, 1878, pp. 1, 2; Dudley to Loud, May 4, 1878, *Letters Received, Dist. of NM,* roll 33, #1047; *Fort Stanton Returns,* roll 1218, post return, April 1878; *Mesilla News,* June 29, 1878, p. 1; Leckie, pp. 196–98; Greenly, pp. 83–84; Ealy, p. 30–31, 33, 34; Wilson, *Merchants, Guns and Money,* pp. 90–91.

19. Dudley to AAAG, July 6, Dudley to AAAG, July 11, Dudley to AAAG, July 11, 1878, *Letters Received, Dist. of NM,* roll 34, #1595, #1647, #1648; *Fort Stanton Returns,* roll 1218, post return, June, 1878; Leckie, pp. 198, 199; Robert M. Utley, "Billy the Kid and the Lincoln County War", *New Mexico Historical Review,* 61 (April 1986): p. 112.

20. Wilson, *Merchants, Guns and Money,* P. 94; Leckie, p. 200.

21. Dudley to AAAG, July 16, Dudley to AAAG, July 18, Dudley to AAAG, July 22, 1878, *Letters Received, Dist. of NM,* roll 34, #1688 enclosures, #1678 enclosures, #1717 enclosures; *Fort Stanton Returns,* roll 1218, post return, July, 1878; *Mesilla News,* July 27, 1878, p. 1; Ealy, pp. 49–50; Leckie, pp. 200–01; Greenly, pp. 85–86.

22. Dudley to AAAG, July 27, Dudley to AAAG, July 18, 1878, *Letters Received, Dist. of NM,* roll 34, #1717, #1678; *Fort Stanton Returns,* roll 1218, post returns, June, July, 1878; *Mesilla News,* July 27, 1878, p. 1; Greenly, pp. 86–87; Leckie, pp. 198, 199, 201–02.

23. Dudley to AAAG, July 22, 1878, *Letters Received, Dist. of NM,* roll 34, #1717; *Fort Stanton Returns,* roll 1218, post return, July 1878; *Mesilla News,* July 27, 1878, p. 1; Leckie, pp. 201–02; Greenly, p. 87; Utley, "Billy the Kid", p. 112; Ealy, pp. 50–52; Wilson, *Merchants, Guns and Money,* P. 97.

24. Ibid.; *Mesilla Valley Independent,* July 27, 1878, p. 3, Aug. 24, 1878, p. 2; Greenly, pp. 88–90; Ealy, pp. 52–55; Leckie, pp. 99–102, 201–02; Wilson, *Merchants, Guns and Money,* p. 183; Barber to Dilton, Nov. 23, 1928, on display in the Tunstall Store,

Lincoln State Monument, Lincoln, New Mexico, (Mrs. Susan E. Barber was formerly Mrs. McSween); "The Lincoln War," the *Mesilla News*, July 27, 1878, p. 1; The *Mesilla Valley Independent*, July 27, 1878, p. 3.

25. Dudley to Loud, May 4, 1878, *Letters Received, Dist. of NM*, roll 33, #1047, This letter had twenty-one enclosures, including statements, affidavits, requests for protection, and requests for troops; Dudley to AAAG, July 13, Dudley to AAAG, July 18, Dudley to AAAG, July 16, Dudley to AAAG, July 22, 1878, *Letters Received, Dist. of NM*, roll 34, #1659, enclosures, #1678, enclosures, #1688, enclosures, #1717, enclosures; *Fort Stanton Returns*, roll 1218, post returns, May–Aug. 1878.

26. Greenly, pp. vi, xii, 82, 84; Leckie, p. 181; Wilson, *Merchants, Guns and Money*, p. 91.

27. *Mesilla Valley Independent*, July 27, 1878, p. 3, Aug. 24, 1878, p. 2, Aug. 31, 1878, p. 2; Dudley to Loud, May 4, 1878, *Letters Received, Dist. of NM*, roll 33 #1047.

28. *Mesilla Valley Independent*, Aug. 31, 1878, p. 2, Sept. 14, 1878, p. 2; Greenly, pp. 90–93; Leckie, pp. 203–05; Wilson, *Merchants, Guns and Money*, pp. 102–06, 107–25.

29. *Population Schedules of the Tenth Census of the United States, 1880*, Microcopy T-9, (NARS), roll 802 (hereafter referred to as *Tenth Census*).

30. *9th Census; 10th Census*; Wilson, *Merchants, Guns and Money*, pp. 130–31.

31. Leckie, pp. 205, 217, 218, 244–45; *Fort Stanton Returns*, roll 1218, post return, Feb. 1880; *Mesilla News*, July 10, 1880, p. 1; Wilson, *Merchants, Guns and Money*, pp. 102–09, 189; Meyers, pp. 35, 37; Stephen H. Lekson, *Nana's Raid: Apache Warfare in New Mexico, 1881*, (El Paso: Texas Western Press, 1969), pp. 38, 47, 145, 147, 150; Hays, pp. 135–36.

32. Wilson, *Merchants, Guns and Money*, pp. 41, 74, 91, 129, 130–32; Miller, *Soldiers and Settlers*, pp. 63, 102–03, 104, 321.

33. *Fort Stanton Returns*, roll 1217, post return, Feb. 1870; *Mesilla News*, Mar. 7, 1874, p. 1; Wilson, *Merchants, Guns and Money*, pp. 66, 76, 130–32, 136; Miller, *Soldiers and Settlers*, pp. 63, 102–04, 317, 321, 344.

34. *Fort Stanton Returns*, roll 1217, post return, Feb. 1870; *Mesilla News*, Mar. 7, 1874, p. 1; Miller, *Soldiers and Settlers*, pp. 102–04, 104, 317, 344; Wilson, *Merchants, Guns and Money*, pp. 66, 76, 130–131, 136.

35. *Mesilla News*, Mar. 4, 1874, p. 1, June 12, 1880, p. 1; *Fort Stanton Returns*, roll 1218, post returns, May–Sept. 1881; Meyers, p. 38; Darlis A. Miller, *The Frontier Army in the Far West: 1860–1900*, (St. Louis: Forum Press, 1979), p. 7; Wilson, *Merchants, Guns and Money*, pp. 130, 147, 160.

36. Leckie, pp. 257–58; Meyers, P. 40, 41–42; Wilson, *Merchants, Guns and Money*, p. 137; Seckler and Hosmer, pp. 29–30; *Fort Stanton Returns*, roll 1218, post returns, Apr. 1880–Dec. 1887; Black to Adjutant General of the Army, Aug. 17, 1896, *Fort Stanton Returns*, roll 1219; Lane, pp. 141–42; S. C. Agnew, *Garrisons of the Regular U.S. Army: New Mexico, 1846–1899*, (Santa Fe: The Press of the Territorian, 1971), p. 1.

37. Stanley, pp. 200, 201–03.

Chapter V

SOME LEISURE ACTIVITIES

The troops and civilians at Fort Stanton had leisure time for relaxation and recreation. Drinking establishments, gambling, and bawdy houses were popular among the troops, but the soldiers also enjoyed other activities. Favorite activities included hunting, fishing, exploring, socials or dances, and the celebration of holidays such as Christmas and New Year's Day. Baseball became popular as the Indian Wars ended and the troops had more leisure time. Fort Stanton and its neighbors, located in a remote and isolated corner of the territory, were interdependent until the waning days of the Indian Wars. When recreational and social activities were undertaken, the community and the fort relied upon each other to help make them successful.[1]

Drinking and gambling were problems throughout the Army and Fort Stanton was no exception. The soldiers at the post occasionally spent too much time at local drinking establishments, or *hog ranches*, and the post commander had to send someone to retrieve them. In November 1859, a very annoyed Capt. Thomas Claiborne, commanding Fort Stanton, found it necessary to send an officer to Mr. Hacket's *hog ranch* to retrieve post absentees. At one time the soldier's daily ration had included one gill, or one quarter-pint, of rum, whisky, or brandy. In 1832 the Secretary of War changed the regulations governing rations, substituting sugar and coffee for the ardent spirits. However, the Commissary and Subsistence Departments still issued whiskey for medicinal purposes and as supplementary rations. In 1865, the Secretary of War tried to curb the soldiers' drinking by prohibiting the

Captain Orsemus Boyd, c. 1868–71
Photo by Nicholas Brown
Courtesy Museum of New Mexico,
Neg. No. 105111

Subsistence and Commissary Departments from providing whiskey.[2]

Whiskey could still be bought at the sutler's store, but it required a note from the post commander, and commanding officers often limited the amount of liquor that could be sold to enlisted men. Soldiers frequently resorted to subterfuge to obtain orders for whiskey. In 1863, some New Mexico Volunteers learned that Col. Christopher Carson could not read manuscript. Obtaining orders for whiskey from the company clerk the men brought them to Carson, representing them as orders for molasses. Claiming they were ill, the soldiers asked Carson to sign the orders. He cheerfully complied and the men bought whiskey from the sutler. Carson later learned of the subterfuge when the sutler, delighted over having recently sold two barrels of whiskey, showed Carson the orders, explaining that they were orders for whiskey. In March 1881, President Rutherford B. Hayes signed a bill prohibiting the sale of whiskey at military installations. This worsened the problem, for troops went into town to drink and got into trouble.[3]

While drinking created problems, the hard drinkers were in the minority and some soldiers did not drink or smoke at all. Hunting and fishing were popular past times and provided variety for the soldier's diet. Col. Augustus V. Kautz liked to fish and once caught 123 fish in a single day in the Rio Bonito. At Fort Stanton the officers' wives particularly enjoyed fishing because fish were so plentiful in the nearby streams that even the poorest fisherwoman was assured of a fine catch.[4]

Often, especially when in the field, soldiers shot game for fresh meat and some commanding officers encouraged hunting as a way to improve soldierly skills. Lt. Orsemus B. Boyd was an outdoorsman and his wife remarked in her diary that they "lived on the 'fat of the land.'" Hunting was in such favor that commanders routinely granted men leave to go hunting. In September 1887, Capt. Benjamin H. Rogers obtained a seven-day leave of absence to go hunting in the Capitan Mountains. The post commander granted Rogers leave again in October for the same purpose. Local civilians often accompanied soldiers taking leave to go hunting. Such junkets occasionally attracted the attention of newspaper columnists. In February 1892, a local newspaper reported that Mr. Barney Caffey, a prominent citizen of Lincoln, and one Sergeant Honey, from Fort Stanton, went duck hunting and returned with fourteen ducks and some glassware. The reporter was unsure whether the men's smiles were "due to the ducks or the contents of the glassware."[5]

In addition to hunting, many of the troops at Fort Stanton enjoyed exploring. In the summer of 1871, Lieutenant Boyd had the post carpenter build a rowboat which he used to explore a cavern, known as Fort Stanton Cave, located about ten miles southeast of the fort. Post Quartermaster Charles H. Conrad accompanied Boyd on the trip. Contemporary records indicate that the cavern was first discovered by troops from Fort Stanton in 1857. However, graffiti inside the cave indicates that at least one individual, who called himself John, explored portions of the cave in 1855. The grotto contains an underground stream and, when the water table is high, a sizeable lake. The men spent several days exploring the cave and discovered a large waterfall. Boyd claimed to have gone eight miles into the cavern. Fort Stanton cave remained an attraction to adventurers throughout the nineteenth century. In the spring of 1892, several civilians from Lincoln, in company with a group of soldiers from the post, made a weekend outing of exploring the cavern.[6] A present day visitor to the cave will encounter the remains of a boat, quite possibly Lieutenant Boyd's, and signatures of such men as Emil Fritz, who inscribed "Five for a bit, E. Fritz," in one of the cave's pas-

Remains of a rowboat in Fort Stanton Cave. Jerry W. Ballard of the Bureau of Land Management guided the author into the cave. It could possibly be the remains of the one Lt. Boyd used to explore the cave. *Courtesy of the author.*

sages. Major Fritz once commanded Fort Stanton and figured prominently in the Lincoln County War. One large formation, known to the Bureau of Land Management people who manage the cave as "Signature Rock," has hundreds of inscriptions proudly proclaiming various Army units, towns, and states from which the scribes hail.

While men like Orsemus Boyd found adventure and excitement in exploration, their wives found a different kind of adventure. Life at isolated army posts was especially difficult for the women. With their husbands frequently away on scout or detached service, they had to make a home and raise a family under primitive conditions with little or no companionship. This task was made more difficult because a soldier's transfer usually necessitated the sale of all or most of the family's household goods due to the prohibitive cost and difficulty of moving them. This was particularly true at the very remote posts such as Fort Stanton. The Army did not provide travel pay or moving expenses and an officer's pay was barely enough to meet expenses while an enlisted man's pay was entirely inadequate. The family generally depended

Signature Rock in Fort Stanton Cave. A careful examination of the photo will reveal numerous names and unit designations left by nineteenth-century visitors to the cave.
Courtesy of the author.

upon merchants in the nearest town to sell their goods or buy new furnishings. If the family moved to a different climate, new clothes were required as well, compounding the strain on the family finances. In December 1889, John C. Delaney, a local business man and post trader, sold household goods at auction for families recently transferred. He announced the auction in the *Lincoln Independent* five days in advance of the sale.[7]

Sometimes a woman arrived at a new post only to find her husband was in the field or on detached duty elsewhere. Lydia Spencer Lane, wife of Lt. William B. Lane, arrived at Fort Stanton in November 1859 with her five-year-old daughter and two servants. Upon her arrival, she learned that her husband had been sent on detached service to participate in a campaign against the Navajos and could be expected to be away for months. Mrs. Lane lived with her sister, whose husband was William's commanding officer, until their husbands returned from detached service. Although Lane described Fort Stanton as a beautiful post and the quarters, which had dirt floors, as the best in the Army, she complained that the fort was so isolated that living there was like being buried alive. Despite the welcome companionship of her sister, Lane was bored. Wild fruit grew abundantly in the region and she relieved the boredom that summer by gathering wild fruit and making pickles and plum jam. Lane lived at Fort Stanton about a year before her husband transferred to Fort Bliss. She was happy to leave Fort Stanton because of the loneliness.[8]

Card parties, an effective means of alleviating boredom, were exciting social occasions for army wives and helped relieve the sense of isolation felt at remote posts. Francis Ann Mullen Boyd, wife of Lt. Orsemus B. Boyd, considered card parties her wildest gaiety. Euchre, whist, casino, cribbage, and pinochle were favorites. Card games were among the most popular off-duty diversions for the soldiers as well. Although the enlisted men preferred money games such as poker, seven-up, and black jack, the money usually ran out shortly after payday and during the remaining time until next payday they played casino, cribbage, and other non-betting games purely for amusement.[9]

News from home was even more stimulating than playing cards and mail was an important link to the rest of the world. In the early 1860s, the mail came monthly and was greatly anticipated because its arrival brought news of home and loved ones. On the scheduled day of arrival some of the women would keep watch and give the alert when the mail wagon was spotted. One of the wives doled out issues of the hometown newspaper one each day and pretended that it was the current news. By 1880 the mail came twice weekly but interruptions in the service still caused consternation. In July 1880, Lt. Walter L. Finley complained to his mother that the rainy season was in full force. The rains had washed out the railroad bridge across the Pecos River and the Rio Bonito had risen twenty feet. As a result of the floods, he had received no mail for two weeks. Finley was expecting some books and was anxious to receive them. Books were very important to inhabitants of western posts. Women went to great lengths to obtain and preserve books. One army wife remarked that a good way to make army quarters look like home was to scatter a few books around. Favorite authors included Schiller, Goethe and Lamartine. Lieutenant Finley asked his mother for the latter's works in French so he could maintain his skill with the language.[10]

When not tending to family matters or reading, army wives often turned to song to relieve the sense of isolation. Lydia Lane's sister had a piano and the officers and their wives entertained themselves by gathering at her quarters and making music. Music was a common form of diversion and socials, or dances, were popular recreational

A musical interlude in the officers' quarters. Lt. John J. "Black Jack" Pershing, on crutches, and friends enjoy a few moments of music from the small-size organ. *Courtesy Museum of New Mexico, Neg. No. 11673.*

activities. Virtually the entire community, civilian and military, attended the socials. As with most military posts of the time, a musical instrument of some kind could almost always be found at Fort Stanton. If musical instruments were not available, the guests kept time by singing, clapping their hands or stamping their feet. Favorite tunes included "Tenting Tonight," "Skip to My Lou," "The Girl I Left Behind Me," and "The Regular Army, O." Holidays, such as Christmas and New Year's Day, were celebrated with lavish socials that included a sumptuous dinner.[11]

In 1869, Lawrence Murphy and Emil Fritz, post sutlers, provided Christmas dinner for a few friends and the officers at Fort Stanton, after which the guests joined the festivities at the fort. Then, on New Year's Day, Murphy and Fritz hosted a dance at the post. They invited the people of the surrounding community and found three fiddlers to provide the music. Colonel Kautz, commanding the post, apparently had the small number of women at the fort in mind when he commented that they "collected a few of the best women in the country" for the affair. Kautz commented further that the musicians were poor, but admitted that they "made quite a noise and the dance passed off pleasantly and merrily." Kautz left the party, still in progress, at three o'clock in the morning. Festivities of this kind often lasted all night and custom required the host, or hostess, to provide breakfast in such cases. Breakfast normally consisted of hot cakes, eggs, side pork, and coffee. The guests usually brought their own cutlery and dishes to help the host with the logistics. Information as to whether Murphy and Fritz provided breakfast is unavailable, but they did provide a midnight supper which Kautz described as excellent.[12]

Sometimes the guests at all night affairs were somewhat critical of the cook's efforts. On May 13, 1881, the daughter of post trader John Delaney married Lt. Dillard H. Clark. Delaney invited the entire community to the reception, providing an expensive and lavish meal. After the celebration one guest described the supper as merely "tolerable." The young officer was more impressed with the dance following the feast. The soldiers erected a platform and covered it with canvas. By the light of the moon, the Fifteenth Infantry regimental band provided music for the party and the dance lasted until the early morning hours. When available, post or regimental bands played an important role in the social activities at remote posts, giving concerts and performing at parties and dances.[13]

The Army did not officially provide for bands in the regimental table of organization and equipment, but each regiment usually had a band. Volunteers selected from the various companies of the regiment made up the regimental bands. Each band paid for its instruments, music, and supplies out of regimental and company funds. These funds came from various sources, principally voluntary contributions by the officers and men and profits from the sale of excess produce from company and post gardens. In June 1881, the Fifteenth Infantry Band selected seven men from Fort Stanton, who promptly transferred to regimental headquarters.[14]

A soggy ride on a pleasant day in the 1880s, as Lt. and Mrs. Richard B. Paddock ride their horses through a stream near Fort Stanton. Mrs. Paddock is riding sidesaddle as was customary. *Courtesy Museum of New Mexico, Neg. No. 11674.*

Regimental bands typically toured the posts where companies of the regiment were stationed, giving concerts and playing for parades. The bands often gave concerts in the nearby communities as well. The regimental band of the Ninth Cavalry was on temporary service at Fort Stanton from May 1877 to March 1878 and was permanently assigned to Fort Stanton in May 1879. However, in October the band went to Santa Fe on detached service. The citizens of Santa Fe were so delighted with the band that city officials asked Col. Edward Hatch, regimental commander, to station the band there permanently. Though regulations prohibited this, the band remained in Santa Fe on detached service until November 1881, when the regiment began leaving New Mexico. While the Ninth's band was in Santa Fe, the regimental band of the Fifteenth Infantry visited the post and was greatly

appreciated. Lt. James McDonough noted that the band gave a significant boost to the garrison's moral.[15]

The positive effect of regimental bands on the soldiers' frame of
mind was underscored by their response to the absence of music. At
Fort Stanton the troops found it particularly galling to have a band that
was not allowed to perform. In August 1881, Lieutenant Clark's bride
became seriously ill and the band was not allowed to play because the
noise aggravated her condition. Though the officers and enlisted men
tolerated the situation, their displeasure was evident. The men became
irritable and discipline declined. Calls were not sounded either, for the
same reason, and the post was nicknamed "*Mes Prisons*" (Our Prison)
by Lt. Walter L. Finley.[16]

An important function of the band was to play for dances, a
favorite off duty activity. Although spectators could make rhythm by
clapping their hands, stamping their feet and singing, musical instruments, if available, were automatically pressed into service. Similarly, if
no women were present the men took turns playing the lady's role.
When women attended, they were always too few in number and were
usually kept busy dancing, sometimes to their displeasure. In February
1861, the owners of a local ranch held a dance at their home near Fort
Stanton for people who were leaving the area, and soldiers and musicians from Fort Stanton attended the dance. Nineteen-year-old Lucy
Mima Wright was much annoyed that evening by the post commander,
Capt. Thomas Claiborne. Claiborne and his adjutant were intoxicated,
and Claiborne pressured Wright to dance with him much against her
wishes. Wright was particularly upset because others then wanted to
dance with her, and she felt that she could not gracefully decline after
dancing with Claiborne. Exhausted, Wright left the affair at 2:00 A.M.
with the festivities going strong. Ironically, Captain Claiborne had complained bitterly to Headquarters just three months before about exces-
sive drinking.[17]

Frances Boyd liked to attend dances and military balls and was disappointed to find that, in 1870, not enough officers' wives lived at Fort
Stanton for them to have dances of their own. Undaunted, Mrs. Boyd
found an acceptable alternative. In the absence of officers' dances, she
and her husband regularly attended the enlisted men's dances. The residents of the region surrounding the fort were always invited to these

affairs and Mrs. Boyd enjoyed the variety and absurdity of the cos-
tumes worn by the guests. On the evening of one soldiers' dance a
severe storm raged, and Boyd feared that the only people in attendance
would be those who lived at the post. Boyd braved the storm and was
pleasantly surprised to find the usual crowd in attendance. The dance
was a success and the stamping of feet, combined with the music and
the howling wind, produced much excitement. The excitement peaked
when a loud crash brought the participants outside in alarm. There
they found the fort's newly constructed flagpole had blown over and
splintered.[18]

Often several dances were held in a single month, as almost any occasion was cause to sponsor a hop. At the May 13 wedding of Lieutenant
Clark, the celebrants danced to the music of the Fifteenth Infantry regimental band until 2:00 in the morning. Just over two weeks later, in the
first week of June, a Miss Willard arrived from Chicago to visit the
Delaneys, and John Delaney sponsored a hop in her honor. A few days
later, Lt. George H. Kinzie and his wife gave a hop to celebrate their seventh wedding anniversary. Lieutenant Finley, who was a ladies man,
escorted Miss Willard to this affair, which also lasted until 2:00 o'clock
the next morning. Finley was very disappointed with Miss Willard
because, though she played the piano, she could not dance.[19]

Enlisted men in the Army held few socials or dances and primarily
found their recreation in sports. Although few post commanders took
an active interest in promoting athletic programs, the Army encouraged sports because they kept the men out of trouble and physically fit.
The competition suited the soldiers' natural propensity to gamble and
sometimes prompted considerable wagering. At Fort Stanton, baseball
became popular in the 1880s, and the fort fielded a team that com-
peted against rivals from the community. In 1891, the Fort Stanton
team played two games against the team from Lincoln, one at Lincoln
and one at the post. Fort Stanton won both games handily.[20]

Sports did not occupy all of the enlisted men's leisure time. By 1886,
the Army was searching for a new mission and had begun encouraging
the professional development of its members. This included the establishment of professional schools and organizations. At most western
army posts, enlisted men established libraries and formed lodges and
unions. The International Order of Good Templars, a temperance

organization, was one of the most widespread, and Masonic lodges and Odd Fellows lodges were also popular. Some of the men at Fort Stanton became involved in civilian professional organizations as well. In December 1889, a group of men organized the Lincoln County Alliance, a chapter of the Territorial Farmers Alliance, in Lincoln. An announcement in the local newspaper listed H. C. Epps and W. L. Breace, both soldiers stationed at Fort Stanton, as Treasurer and County Lecturer, respectively. In February 1892, the enlisted men at the fort formed a Regular Army and Navy Union garrison. The new organization listed its officers in an announcement in the *Lincoln Independent*.[21]

As can be seen, Fort Stanton and the community it protected depended upon each other not only for defense and subsistence, but also for social interaction. Activities such as suppers and dances were fashionable but the post community was small and the success of a party or dance depended on the attendance of people from the civilian community. On the other hand, the civilian community lacked resources such as a band. Thus the civilian and post communities cooperated in such endeavors as weddings and hops. As the Indian Wars came to a close, sports activities and professional organizations became more prevalent. A successful baseball team at the post could hardly be formed without worthy opponents. The community of Lincoln, among others, met this requirement. The soldiers had once been civilians and would return to civilian life at the end of their terms of service. Thus, civilian professional organizations, such as the Territorial Farmers Alliance, found support among the soldiers at the post. Throughout the tenure of Fort Stanton as an active Army station, even as social requirements changed, the fort and the surrounding community relied upon each other for satisfactory social and leisure time activities.

Notes to Chapter V

1. Rickey, pp. 54–55, 168–169; Wilson p. 29, 30, 31; Claiborne to Wilkins, Nov. 16, 1859, *Letters Received, Dept. of NM,* roll 9, C33; Wallace, pp. 245, 247.

2. Claiborne to Wilkins, Nov. 16, 1859, *Letters Received, Dept. of NM,* roll 9, C33; Rickey, pp. 161, 163; Francis Paul Prucha, *Broadax and Bayonet: The role of the United States Army in the Development of the Northwest, 1815–1860,* (Lincoln: University of Nebraska Press, 1953), pp. 48–50, 50n, 153, 153n.

3. Rickey, pp. 159–63, 168, 200; Leckie, pp. 28–29; Claiborne to Wilkins, Nov. 16, 1859, *Letters Received, Dept. of NM,* roll 9, C33; *The Mesilla Valley Independent,* Sept. 8, 1877, p. 1; Guild and Carter, pp. 226–28.

4. Rickey, pp. 54–56, 120, 251; Wallace, p. 247; Boyd, pp. 164–65.

5. Rickey, pp. 54–56, 120, 251; Wallace, p. 247; Boyd, pp. 164–65; Monroe Lee Billington, *New Mexico's Buffalo Soldiers, 1866–1900,* (Niwot, CO: University Press of Colorado, 1991) p. 155; *Fort Stanton Returns,* roll 1218, post returns, Sept.–Nov. 1887; *Lincoln Independent,* Feb. 19, 1892, p. 4.

6. *Fort Stanton Returns,* roll 1217, post returns, Apr. 1870–Oct. 1871; Henry James, "The Mysterious Fort Stanton Cave," *New Mexico Trails,* 7 (June 1954): 8–9; Boyd, p. viii; Royce Bellinger and Dick Smith, "Preliminary Report of Investigations of Fort Stanton Cave near Fort Stanton, New Mexico," National Speleological Society, Permian Basin Speleological Society, 1959, copy at Lincoln County Heritage Trust Museum, Lincoln, New Mexico; *The Lincoln Independent,* Feb. 19, 1892, p. 4; Photographic exploration of the cave by the author, guided by Mr. Jerry Ballard, of the Bureau of Land Management, June 20, 1997.

7. Lane, pp. 152–53; Brown, pp. 47–48; *Lincoln Independent,* Dec. 6, 1889, p. 3.

8. Lane, pp. 62, 64, 67, 149; *Fort Stanton Returns,* roll 1216, post returns, Feb., Nov.–Dec., 1859; *8th Census.*

9. Boyd, p. 166; Rickey, pp. 208–09.

10. Finley to Mother, July 26, Sept. 28, Nov. 30, 1880, Feb. 20, Feb.

26, Aug. 31, 1881, Copies at Lincoln County Historical Society archives, Lincoln, New Mexico (hereafter referred to as LCHS); Dee Brown, *The Gentle Tamers: Women of the Old West*, (Lincoln: University of Nebraska Press, 1958), p. 152; Lane, pp. 62, 64–65, 67.

11. Lane, p. 65; Brown, p. 152; Rickey, pp. 189, 192.

12. Brown, pp. 152–53; Rickey, pp. 189, 191–92; Diary of General Augustus V. Kautz, quoted in Wallace, pp. 245–46.

13. Finley to Mother, May 20, 1881, copy at LCHS; McDonough to Wife, Nov. 27, 1880, copy at LCHS; *Fort Stanton Returns*, roll 1218, post returns, Oct. 1880–June 1881.

14. Leckie, pp. 17, 50, 179: Rickey, p. 198; Billington, pp. 116–20; *Fort Stanton Returns*, roll 1218, post returns, June–July 1880.

15. Billington, pp. 116–20; *Fort Stanton Returns*, roll 1217–1218, post returns, May 1877–March 1878, May–Oct. 1879, Nov. 1881; McDonough to Wife, Nov. 27, 1880, copy at LCHS; Finley to Mother, May 20, Finley to Mother, Aug. 29, 1881, copy at LCHS.

16. Finley to Mother, May 20, Finley to Mother, Aug. 29, 1881, copy at LCHS.

17. Rickey, pp. 198–200; Brown, pp. 152–53; Diary of Lucy Mima Wright, transcript at Lincoln County Heritage Trust Museum, Lincoln, New Mexico; Claiborne to Wilkins, Nov. 16, 1859, *Letters Received, Dept. of NM*, roll 9, C33.

18. Boyd, pp. 166–67.

19. Finley to Mother, Mar. 18, Finley to Mother, May 20, Finley to Mother, June 12, 1881, copy at LCHS.

20. Rickey, pp. 186, 188; Wilson, *Merchants, Guns and Money*, p. 155.

21. Gary D. Ryan and Timothy K. Nenninger, eds., *Soldiers and Civilians, the U. S. Army and the American People*, (Washington, DC: NARS, 1987), pp. 28–31, 34; Russell F. Weigley, *The American Way of War: A History of United States Military Strategy and Policy*, (Bloomington: Indiana University Press, 1973), pp. 167–69; Edward M. Coffman, *The Old Army: A Portrait of the American Army in Peacetime, 1784–1898*, (New York: Oxford University Press, 1986), p. 282; Rickey, pp. 194–96, 209–10; *Lincoln Independent*, Dec. 6, 1889, p. 2, Feb. 19, 1892, p. 4.

CONCLUSION

In its forty-one years of existence as a military post Fort Stanton fostered settlement in a remote district of southeast New Mexico by providing protection from Indians and a market for the goods produced by settlers in the area. The region in which Fort Stanton stood was fertile farmland, covered with lush grasses, and rich in game and minerals. Building Fort Stanton took several years and problems abounded, but even before construction began settlers started moving into the area. They came with the expectation that the fort would provide security from Indian depredations and that the fertile soil and abundant streams would provide a prosperous future. By building roads to the fort for supply and communication, the Army further facilitated settlement in the region. Aided by these roads the area grew rapidly, but even with the Army-built roads the remoteness made the cost of shipping goods prohibitive. Because of this, a symbiotic relationship soon developed wherein the farmers and ranchers in the district provided hay, grain, and other provisions required by the post and the fort provided the market and security required by the settlers.

Settlers in the district produced substantial crops, even in times of drought, and the garrison at the fort maintained peace with the Mescalero Indians while the area continued to grow and prosper. The outbreak of the Civil War and the resultant reassignment of the troops, demonstrated the importance of the fort in fostering settlement and growth in the region. When the Army abandoned the post, the Mescaleros began raiding and the settlers abandoned their holdings. When the Army reopened Fort Stanton, settlers returned in spite of the difficulties the garrison was having in suppressing Indian raids. As the soldiers gradually gained mastery of the region, Indian problems lessened. Immigration to the district was greater than before the Civil War and the population grew to record proportions.

As the population grew and communications improved, the economic importance of the post diminished and the symbiosis dissolved. The coming of the railroad opened significantly wider markets to the inhabitants of the area and brought cheaper produce from Kansas and other regions. Because of this, local farmers and ranchers began growing fruit and alfalfa for a distant market instead of corn and wheat for the local military.

With the Mescaleros living peacefully on a reservation, and the Indian wars drawing to a close, the commanders of Fort Stanton tried to accomplish their mission to provide security by involving their troops in civil affairs, sometimes with disastrous results. By the late 1880s the post no longer served an important military function and the railroad had minimized the fort's economic significance to the community. The Army concluded that the fort had served its purpose and closed Fort Stanton in 1896.

When the Army abandoned Fort Stanton, it did not demolish the post. In 1899 Fort Stanton became the first federal hospital exclusively for the treatment of tuberculosis when President McKinley set the fort aside for use by the Merchant Marine. During World War Two, the federal government interned the crew of the German cruise ship *Columbia,* sunk in the Caribbean in 1939, at the hospital. Later, after the United States entered the war and occupied North Africa, the government also kept German prisoners of war at the fort. The federal government decided to close the Fort Stanton Merchant Marine Hospital, which included more than eighty-five buildings, in 1953. The government transferred the hospital to the state of New Mexico and the New Mexico Department of Public Welfare took charge of the hospital that same year. By the 1960's the volume of TB patients had fallen significantly, the result of new drugs and treatments for TB. In 1966 the New Mexico Department of Health converted the fort for use by the Los Lunas Hospital and Training School for the Mentally Disadvantaged. The old army post continued to serve the New Mexico community in that capacity until 1995.

But, that still did not end the story of the fort's service to the com-

These former barracks, made of stone, are still serviceable today, as the automobiles and chain-link fence indicate. *Courtesy of the author.*

munity. In 1995 the Department of Health closed the hospital facility and the state began searching for someone to lease the property. The closure sparked serious efforts by the community to preserve the fort as an historical site. Citizens' groups banned together to preserve the fort and the New Mexico legislature passed House Bill 926 in April of 2003 to establish and fund a Fort Stanton Development Commission to establish the Fort as an historical site and living history museum. Meanwhile, in 1996, the State of New Mexico Department of Corrections converted the fort into a minimum-security detention facility for women, which resided at the fort until 2000. Currently, Amity Foundation, Incorporated, under a contract with the Department of Corrections, operates a drug and alcohol rehabilitation center for parolees at the facility.

Modern visitors entering Fort Stanton can envision themselves in the nineteenth century, looking at a post in the days of the "Old Army." Visitors can see the grass-covered parade ground and the original stone buildings that surround it. With the exception of the addition of wooden floors, these buildings are largely as they were when the fort was closed over one hundred years ago. Even some of the adobe stables are still standing, showing the ravages of weather and time. Seemingly out of place, a 1940's-vintage anti-aircraft artillery piece stands near the entrance, between the road and the stables, as a monument to the veterans of WWII. The fort also boasts a volunteer fire department, and an ancient 1916 American LaFrance fire engine. The department serves the surrounding community and is manned by staff and residents of the Amity facility. The fort grounds also house the Marine cemetery, where the patients of the Marine Hospital are buried. Down in the lower corner of the cemetery, lie the graves of four of the *Columbia* crew who died while interned at Fort Stanton.

This is Fort Stanton Hospital, c. 1886–89. Each room had a fireplace. Although the post had telegraph and telephone, electricity did not arrive before the post closed, hence the gas lamps. *Photo by J.R. Riddle, courtesy Museum of New Mexico, Neg. No. 11678.*

BIBLIOGRAPHY

Primary Sources

National Archives and Records Service, Washington, DC.

Department of New Mexico, Letters Received, Record Group 98, microfilm copy at New Mexico State Archives and Records Center, Santa Fe.

Department of New Mexico Letters Sent and Received, Quartermaster General Records, Commissary General Records, All New Mexico, 1848–1861. Record Groups 98, 92, and 192, microfilm copy at New Mexico State Archives and Records Center, Santa Fe.

Interior Department Appointment Papers; Territory of New Mexico, 1850–1907. Record Group 48, "Records of the Office of the Secretary of the Interior," Microcopy M750, 18 rolls.

Letters Received, Fort Stanton, RG 98, Letters Received and Sent, Forts Garland, Conrad, Craig, Stanton, Union. Microfilm copy at New Mexico State Archives and Records Center, Santa Fe.

Letters Received by Headquarters, District of New Mexico, September 1865 to August 1890, Record Group 393, Microcopy M1088, rolls 1–10.

Letters Sent by the 9th Military Department, the Department of New Mexico, and the District of New Mexico, 1849–1890, Record Group 393, Microcopy M1072, 48 rolls.

Letters Sent by Assistant Commissary of Subsistence Berney, Fort Stanton New Mexico Only, Oct. 1862–May 1863. Record Group 393, microfilm copy at New Mexico State University Library.

Population Schedules of the Seventh Census of the United States, 1850, Microcopy T-6, roll 169.

Population Schedules of the Eighth Census of the United States, 1860, Microcopy 653, roll 714.

Population Schedules of the Ninth Census of the United States, 1870, Microcopy 593, roll 898.

Population Schedules of the Tenth Census of the United States, 1880, Microcopy T-9, roll 802.

Records of the New Mexico Superintendency of Indian Affairs, 1849–80, Microcopy T-21, 30 rolls.

Register of Letters Received and Letters Received by Headquarters, Department of New Mexico, 1854–1865. Record Group 393 Microcopy M1120, 30 rolls.

Returns from U. S. Military Posts, 1800-1916: Fort Stanton New Mexico Only. Record Group 393, Microcopy M617, 4 rolls.

Government Documents

United States Army. *The War of the Rebellion: A Compilation of the Official Records of the Union and Confed-erate Armies,* 128 vols. Washington, DC: United States Printing Office, 1880-1901.

United States War Department, Surgeon General's Office, "Report on Barracks and Hospitals with Descriptions of Military Posts," Circular 4, Washington, DC: United States Government Printing Office, 1870.

Congresssional Documents & Reports

Senate Executive Document 23, Report of The Secretary of War, "Report of Lt. J. W. Albert of his examination of New Mexico in the Years 1846–1847", 30th Congress, 1st Session. (Lincoln, NM: Lincoln County Heritage Trust Facsimile Reprint, n.d.).

Senate Report Number 156, "Condition of Indian Tribes," 39th Congress, 2nd Session.

Diaries

Alexander, Eveline M. *Cavalry Wife: The Dairy of Eveline M. Alexander, 1866–1867*. Sandra L. Myres, ed., Col-lege Station: Texas A&M University Press, 1977.

Bennett, James A. *Forts and Forays: James A. Bennett, A Dragoon in New Mexico, 1850–1856*. Clinton E. Brooks and Frank D. Reeve, eds., Albuquerque: Universi-ty of New Mexico Press, 1948.

Boyd, Frances Anne Mullen. *Cavalry Life in Tent and Field*. New York: J. S. Tait, 1894; repr., Lincoln: Universi-ty of Nebraska Press, 1982.

Ealy, Taylor F. *Missionaries, Outlaws, and Indians: Taylor F. Ealy at Lincoln and Zuni, 1878–1881*. Norman J. Bender, ed., Albuquerque: University of New Mexico Press, 1984.

Farmer, James E. *My Life with the Army in the West: Memoirs of James E. Farmer, 1858–1898*. Dale F. Giese, ed., Santa Fe: Jack D. Rittenhouse, 1967; repr., Silver City, NM: Dale F. Giese, 1993.

Lane, Lydia Spencer. *I Married a Soldier: Or Old Days in the Old Army*. Philadelphia: Lippincott Co., 1893; repr., Albuquerque: Horn and Wallace, 1964.

Newspapers

Santa Fe Daily New Mexican

New Orleans Daily Picayune

Lincoln Independent

Mesilla Miner

Mesilla News

Mesilla Times

Mesilla Valley Independent

Santa Fe Weekly Gazette

Santa Fe Weekly New Mexican

Oral Histories

Old Lincoln County Pioneer Stories: Interviews from the WPA Writer's Project. Lincoln, NM: Lincoln County Historical Society Publications, 1994.

Museums & Archives

Lincoln County Heritage Trust Museum files, Lincoln, New Mexico.

Lincoln County Historical Society archives, Lincoln, New Mexico.

Lincoln State Monument, Lincoln, New Mexico.

Books & Periodicals

Books

Agnew, S. C. *Garrisons of the Regular U. S. Army: New Mexico.* Santa Fe: The Press of the Territorian, 1971.

Beck, Warren A. and Ynez D. Haase. *Historical Atlas of New Mexico.* Norman: University of Oklahoma Press, 1969.

Billington, Monroe Lee. *New Mexico's Buffalo Soldiers, 1866–1900.* Niwot, CO: University Press of Colorado, 1991.

Brown, Dee. *The Gentle Tamers: Women of the Old West.* Lincoln: University of Nebraska Press, 1958.

Coffman, Edward M. *The Old Army: A Portrait of the American Army in Peacetime, 1784–1898.* New York: Oxford University Press, 1986.

Cummings, Billy Charles Patrick. *Frontier Parish: Recovered Catholic History of Lincoln County, 1860–1884.* Lincoln, NM: Lincoln County Historical Society Publications, 1995.

Faulk, Odie B. *The Geronimo Campaign.* New York: Oxford University Press, 1969.

Frazer, Robert W. *Forts and Supplies: The role of the Army in the Economy of the Southwest, 1846–1861.* Albuquerque: University of New Mexico Press, 1983.

Giese, Dale F. *Forts of New Mexico: Echoes of the Bugle*. Silver City: n.p., 1991.

Guild, Thelma S. and Harvey L. Carter. *Kit Carson: A Pattern for Heroes*. Lincoln: University of Nebraska Press, 1984.

Kelly, Lawrence C. *Navajo Roundup: Selected Correspondence of Kit Carson's Expedition Against the Navajo, 1863–1865*. Boulder, CO: The Pruett Publishing Company, 1970.

Leckie, William H. *The Buffalo Soldiers: A Narrative of the Negro Cavalry in the West*. Norman: University of Oklahoma Press, 1967.

Lekson, Stephen H. *Nana's Raid: Apache Warfare in Southern New Mexico, 1881*. El Paso: Texas Western Press, 1987.

Meyers, Lee C. *Fort Stanton, New Mexico: The Military Years, 1855–1896*. Lincoln, NM: Lincoln County Historical Society Publications, 1983.

Miller, Darlis A. *The Frontier Army in the Far West: 1860–1900*. St. Louis, MO: Forum Press, 1979.

———. *The California Column in New Mexico*. Albuquerque: University of New Mexico Press, 1982.

———. *Soldiers and Settlers: Military Supply in the Southwest, 1861–1885*. Albuquerque: University of New Mexico Press, 1989.

Prucha, Francis Paul. *Broadax and Bayonet: The Role of the United States Army in the Development of the North-west, 1815–1860*. Lincoln: University of Nebraska Press, 1953.

Rickey, Don Jr. *Forty Miles a Day on Beans and Hay: The Enlisted Soldier Fighting the Indian Wars*. Norman: University of Oklahoma Press, 1963.

Ryan, Gary D. and Timothy K. Nenninger, eds. *Soldiers and Civilians, the U. S. Army and the American People*. Washington, DC: National Archives and Records Service, 1987.

Seckler, Herb and Ken Hosmer. *Ruidoso Countryside: The Early Days*. Ruidoso: Herb Seckler and Ken Hosmer, 1987.

Stanley, Frances. *The Antonchico New Mexico Story*. s.l., s.n., n.d..

————. *Fort Stanton*. Pampa, TX: Pampa Print Shop, 1964.

Thomas, Alfred B. and Averam B. Bender. *Apache Indians*, vol. XI. New York: Garland Publishing Inc., 1974.

Utley, Robert M. *Fort Union National Monument*. Washington, DC: National Park Service, U.S. Department of the Interior, 1962.

————. *Frontiersmen in Blue: The United States Army and the Indian, 1848–1865*. Lincoln: University of Nebras-ka Press, 1967.

————. *Frontier Regulars: The United States Army and the Indian, 1866–1891*. New York: Macmillan Publishing Co., Inc., 1973.

————. *Fort Union and the Santa Fe Trail*. El Paso: Texas Western Press, 1989.

Weigley, Russell F. *The American Way of War: A History of United States Military Strategy and Policy*. Blooming-ton: Indiana University Press, 1973.

Wilson, John P. *Merchants, Guns and Money: The Story of Lincoln County and Its Wars*. Santa Fe: Museum of New Mexico Press, 1987.

Periodicals

Bender, A. B. "Frontier Defense in the Territory of New Mexico, 1853–1861," *New Mexico Historical Review* 9 (October 1934): 345–374.

Greer, Richard R. "Origins of the Foreign-Born Population of New Mexico During the Territorial Period," *New Mexico Historical Review* 17 (October 1942): 281–287.

James, Henry. "The Mysterious Fort Stanton Cave," *New Mexico Sun Trails* 7 (June 1954): 8–9.

Miller, Darlis A. "Carleton's California Column: A Chapter in New Mexico's Mining History," *New Mexico Historical Review* 53 (January 1978): 5–38.

Rasch, P. J. "The Tularosa Ditch War," *New Mexico Historical Review* 43 (July 1968): 229–235.

Utley, Robert M. "Billy the Kid and the Lincoln County War," *New Mexico Historical Review* 61 (April 1986): 93–120.

Wallace, Andrew. "Duty in the District of New Mexico: A Military Memoir," *New Mexico Historical Review* 50 (July 1975): 231–262.

Wilson, John P. "Whiskey at Fort Fillmore: A Story of the Civil War," *New Mexico Historical Review* 68 (April 1993): 109–132.

Theses & Papers

Theses

Greenly, Dee Dwight. "The Military Career of Nathan Augus-tus Monroe Dudley, 1843-1889." Master's thesis, New Mexico State University, 1986.

Hays, Kelly R. "Fort Stanton: A History of its Relation-ship with the Mescalero Apaches." Master's thesis, New Mexico State University, 1988.

Miller, Darlis A. "General James Henry Carleton in New Mexico." Master's thesis, New Mexico State Universi-ty, 1970.

Unpublished papers

Bellinger, Royce and Dick Smith. "Preliminary Report of Investigations of Fort Stanton Cave Near Fort Stan-ton, New Mexico." National Speleological Society, 1959. Copy at Lincoln County Heritage Trust Museum, Lincoln, New Mexico.

Gorney, Carole. "Roots in Lincoln: A History of Fort Stanton Hospital." Submitted to the New Mexico State Planning Office by the Director of New Mexico Depart-ment of Hospitals and Institutions, July 1969. Copy at Lincoln County Heritage Trust Museum, Lincoln, New Mexico.

Lincoln County Historical Trust Museum. "Chronological History of Fort Stanton." Lincoln: Lincoln County Historical Trust, n.d

INDEX

143